Grover
Cleveland

Henry F. Graff

Grover
Cleveland

THE AMERICAN PRESIDENTS

ARTHUR M. SCHLESINGER, JR., GENERAL EDITOR

Times Books

HENRY HOLT AND COMPANY, NEW YORK

Times Books
Henry Holt and Company, LLC
Publishers since 1866
175 Fifth Avenue
New York, New York 10010
www.henryholt.com

Frontispiece: President Grover Cleveland © Oscar White/CORBIS

LIBRARY OF CONGRESS CATALOGING-IN-PUBLICATION DATA
Graff, Henry F. (Henry Franklin), 1921–
Grover Cleveland / Henry F. Graff.—1st ed.
    p. cm. — (The American presidents series)
Includes bibliographical references and index.
ISBN-13: 978-0-8050-6923-5
ISBN-10: 0-8050-6923-2
1. Cleveland, Grover, 1837–1908. 2. Presidents—United States—Biography.
I. Title. II. American presidents series (Times Books (Firm))
E697.G73 2002
973.8'5'092—dc21
[B]   2002020315

First Edition 2002

Printed in the United States of America
3   5   7   9   10   8   6   4   2

For Molly, Betsy, Marshall, Nathaniel, and Sarah

Contents

Editor's Note

THE AMERICAN PRESIDENCY

The president is the central player in the American political order. That would seem to contradict the intentions of the Founding Fathers. Remembering the horrid example of the British monarchy, they invented a separation of powers in order, as Justice Brandeis later put it, "to preclude the exercise of arbitrary power." Accordingly, they divided the government into three allegedly equal and coordinate branches—the executive, the legislative, and the judiciary.

But a system based on the tripartite separation of powers has an inherent tendency toward inertia and stalemate. One of the three branches must take the initiative if the system is to move. The executive branch alone is structurally capable of taking that initiative. The Founders must have sensed this when they accepted Alexander Hamilton's proposition in the Seventieth *Federalist* that "energy in the executive is a leading character in the definition of good government." They thus envisaged a strong president—but within an equally strong system of constitutional accountability. (The term *imperial presidency* arose in the 1970s to describe the situation when the balance between power and accountability is upset in favor of the executive.)

The American system of self-government thus comes to focus in the presidency—"the vital place of action in the system," as

Woodrow Wilson put it. Henry Adams, himself the great-grandson and grandson of presidents as well as the most brilliant of American historians, said that the American president "resembles the commander of a ship at sea. He must have a helm to grasp, a course to steer, a port to seek." The men in the White House (thus far only men, alas) in steering their chosen courses have shaped our destiny as a nation.

Biography offers an easy education in American history, rendering the past more human, more vivid, more intimate, more accessible, more connected to ourselves. Biography reminds us that presidents are not supermen. They are human beings too, worrying about decisions, attending to wives and children, juggling balls in the air and putting on their pants one leg at a time. Indeed, as Emerson contended, "There is properly no history; only biography."

Presidents serve us as inspirations, and they also serve us as warnings. They provide bad examples as well as good. The nation, the Supreme Court has said, has "no right to expect that it will always have wise and humane rulers, sincerely attached to the principles of the Constitution. Wicked men, ambitious of power, with hatred of liberty and contempt of law, may fill the place once occupied by Washington and Lincoln."

The men in the White House express the ideal and the values, the frailties and the flaws, of the voters who send them there. It is altogether natural that we should want to know more about the virtues and the vices of the fellows we have elected to govern us. As we know more about them, we will know more about ourselves. The French political philosopher Joseph de Maistre said, "Every nation has the government it deserves."

At the start of the twenty-first century, forty-two men have made it to the oval office. (George W. Bush is counted our forty-third president, because Grover Cleveland, who served nonconsecutive terms, is counted twice.) Of the parade of presidents, a dozen or so lead the polls periodically conducted by historians and political scientists. What makes a great president?

Great presidents possess, or are possessed by, a vision of an ideal America. Their passion, as they grasp the helm, is to set the ship of state on the right course toward the port they seek. Great presidents also have a deep psychic connection with the needs, anxieties, dreams of people. "I do not believe," said Wilson, "that any man can lead who does not act . . . under the impulse of a profound sympathy with those whom he leads—a sympathy which is insight—an insight which is of the heart rather than of the intellect."

"All of our great presidents," said Franklin D. Roosevelt, "were leaders of thought at a time when certain ideas in the life of the nation had to be clarified." So Washington incarnated the idea of federal union, Jefferson and Jackson the idea of democracy, Lincoln union and freedom, Cleveland rugged honesty. Theodore Roosevelt and Wilson, said FDR, were both "moral leaders, each in his own way and his own time, who used the presidency as a pulpit."

To succeed, presidents must not only have a port to seek but they must convince Congress and the electorate that it is a port worth seeking. Politics in a democracy is ultimately an educational process, an adventure in persuasion and consent. Every president stands in Theodore Roosevelt's bully pulpit.

The greatest presidents in the scholars' rankings, Washington, Lincoln, and Franklin Roosevelt, were leaders who confronted and overcame the republic's greatest crises. Crisis widens presidential opportunities for bold and imaginative action. But it does not guarantee presidential greatness. The crisis of secession did not spur Buchanan or the crisis of depression spur Hoover to creative leadership. Their inadequacies in the face of crisis allowed Lincoln and the second Roosevelt to show the difference individuals make to history. Still, even in the absence of first-order crisis, forceful and persuasive presidents—Jefferson, Jackson, James K. Polk, Theodore Roosevelt, Harry Truman, John F. Kennedy, Ronald Reagan, George W. Bush—are able to impose their own priorities on the country.

The diverse drama of the presidency offers a fascinating set of tales. Biographies of American presidents constitute a chronicle of wisdom and folly, nobility and pettiness, courage and cunning, forthrightness and deceit, quarrel and consensus. The turmoil perennially swirling around the White House illuminates the heart of the American democracy.

It is the aim of the American Presidents series to present the grand panorama of our chief executives in volumes compact enough for the busy reader, lucid enough for the student, authoritative enough for the scholar. Each volume offers a distillation of character and career. I hope that these lives will give readers some understanding of the pitfalls and potentialities of the presidency and also of the responsibilities of citizenship. Truman's famous sign—"The buck stops here"—tells only half the story. Citizens cannot escape the ultimate responsibility. It is in the voting booth, not on the presidential desk, that the buck finally stops.

—Arthur M. Schlesinger, Jr.

Grover
Cleveland

Prologue

When Grover Cleveland was born on March 18, 1837, Andrew Jackson had just left the White House and Martin Van Buren was in his place. Three months later, on the other side of the Atlantic, an unknown eighteen-year-old princess called Victoria, granddaughter of George III, became queen of England. When Cleveland died on June 24, 1908, Victoria had given her name to an age that witnessed the flourishing of history's greatest empire, one on which the sun was said never to set. The president of the United States was Theodore Roosevelt, who had helped excite in Americans their own lust for colonial "possessions." Van Buren's time at the helm was brief and undistinguished, but along with Jackson he had helped usher in the era of the common man. So it was that the rising power of the people as the rightful stewards of their own affairs, and the countervailing power of the state fostering overseas imperialism, were contradictory forces at work in Cleveland's lifetime that would notably shape his public career and reputation.

1

Early Years

Cleveland was baptized Stephen Grover, but he never used the Stephen after he grew up. He was the fifth of the nine children and third son of the Reverend Richard Falley Cleveland and Ann Neal, a native of Baltimore. There her father, Abner Neal, made a living as a bookseller and publisher of law books. He and his family had emigrated recently from Ireland, possibly fleeing the consequences of involvement in the 1798 uprising against the British crown. Ann's mother, Barbara Reel, was a Quaker of German background from Germantown, Pennsylvania. The new baby, then, like his siblings, would be regarded as a "typical" American—an amalgam of English, Irish, and German stock.

The father of the future president was a Yale graduate, class of 1824, ordained into the Presbyterian ministry at the Princeton Theological Seminary in 1829. Having fallen in love with Ann Neal while he was a tutor in Baltimore, he and she were married the same year. The fledgling minister's maiden pastorate was the First Congregational Church of Windham, Connecticut. To the dismay of her husband's new flock, his bride arrived on the scene accompanied by a black maid, and garbed in a flashy dress, her wrists jangling with bracelets. Quickly, though, she sent the maid back to Baltimore, took off the jewelry, and began comporting herself in less dazzling fashion as a devoted helpmate to her husband.

Richard Cleveland worked so hard in his post that he fell ill. Friends, believing that he needed a change of scene, obtained a pulpit for him in a Presbyterian church in Portsmouth, Virginia. The lively Ann was pleased that once more she could put on her jewelry and dress as she pleased. Two years later, in 1835, Reverend Richard was called to the pastorate of the Presbyterian congregation in Caldwell, New Jersey. There he came under the influence of the Reverend Steven Grover, an aging minister, long associated with the church, who was filling in in the pulpit until the Clevelands got there. When their fifth child arrived soon afterward, it seemed apt to name him for the admired elderly cleric.

The tiny village of Caldwell, where Stephen Grover Cleveland came into the world, was originally known as Horseneck. It had been renamed in 1798 in honor of James Caldwell, a minister whose exploits during the Revolution in support of Washington and his troops had earned him the sobriquet of "Fighting Parson." Located just northwest of Newark on the Passaic River, Caldwell had a population of no more than a thousand in the 1830s, having doubled in size since1800. It enjoyed a reputation for having such salubrious air that physicians recommended to their patients locating there as a cure-all for a medley of ailments. Like many such pin-dot communities, its coterie of farm families were supplied by a general store, a sawmill, a distillery, a local cider mill, and a blacksmith's shop. But its history was unique, and an inquisitive family like the Clevelands must have gloried in what they learned of it. The very road on which the Cleveland two-story frame house stood, now known as Bloomfield Avenue, had been the scene of the well-remembered Horseneck Riots of 1745, which pitted the settlers against the proprietors of New Jersey over land titles, in what may be considered one of the earliest rebellions against the Crown.

As isolated and sleepy as small towns still were in the 1830s, a new epoch was emerging, although it was only in retrospect that people could know this was so. More than ever before, Americans—not only the Cleveland family—were on the move. After the Erie Canal was opened in New York in 1825, a canal-building frenzy gripped the country. By the time the Panic of 1837 put an end to the canal boom, it was possible to travel along internal waterways from New York to New Orleans. All in all, three thousand miles of canals crisscrossed the country, mostly in the North. Yet the horse remained ubiquitous for most transportation until well into the next century. It was the railroad, though, its route not bound by the availability of rivers and lakes, that became the great binder of the nation, its tracks serving as giant straps connecting the sections better than ever before. Whereas there were twenty-eight hundred miles of rail in 1840, a decade later there were nine thousand. It was plain to see that the "cars," as railroads soon were called, remade every town center that they reached. Their arrival on schedule forced people to be mindful of the clock. Everything, it appeared, was being done in "railroad time" now, and life was noticeably speeding up. Henry David Thoreau, who was fascinated by the Iron Horse, "breathing fire and smoke from its nostrils," asked even as he knew the answer: "Do [people] not talk and think faster in the depot than in the stage office?" New states constantly coming into the Union added every few years to the number of stars in the flag: Arkansas in 1836, Michigan the following year, Florida and Texas in 1845, Wisconsin in 1848, and California in 1850.

It is safe to guess that the Clevelands, even in their quiet little town, felt the vibrations from these developments. But their way of living was no different from those of their eighteenth-century forebears. When Grover was four years old, his father was called as pastor to yet another church. This time the family moved to Fayetteville, New York, a snug and beautiful village in the western part of the state near Syracuse, enriched by the trade flowing on the Erie Canal. Settled in 1792, it was named for the immortal French hero of the Revolution, the Marquis de Lafayette. The handsome Greek Revival homes that still stand there testify to the prosperity of the local quarries, mills, and farms. Here Cleveland, known to his friends as Big Steve, attended the Fayetteville Academy. Full of drive and dash, the boy was serious in his studies although he participated in pranks. He received excellent training in mathematics and Latin, and he took to his work apparently with self-confidence. He began to enjoy fishing as a hobby, and it would give him pleasure throughout his life. There were few other diversions, and the day practically ended at nightfall, even though the new oil lamps were extending the hours for reading. The penny press was emerging, marked by the appearance of the *Sun* in New York City in 1833. A few years later Horace Greeley, a transplanted Vermonter, established the *Tribune*, which in its weekly form became a staple in rural homes. Nevertheless, most small towns were still not touched by the force of daily news. Indoor plumbing, ready-made furniture, and balloon-frame houses were beginning to change domestic habits in some places, but these improvements were beyond the reach of most people, including the Clevelands.

Although they would remain impecunious like most clerical households, its members surely entertained no feeling of inferiority or deprivation. Pride of ancestry always buttressed their sense of themselves. The first Cleveland, Moses, a child of eleven, who spelled the name Cleaveland, had arrived in Massachusetts around 1634 from Ipswich, Suffolk County, England, as an apprentice indentured to a joiner. He was accompanied by his brother Aaron. Prosperity soon rewarded the youths' diligence. Moses's great-grandson, also an Aaron Cleveland, was Grover's great-great-grandfather, and a friend of Benjamin Franklin. In fact, he had died in Franklin's house in Philadelphia while seeking medical treatment in the city. It was he who dropped the letter "a" from the family surname. A Harvard alumnus, he took holy orders as a Presbyterian but, having converted to Episcopalianism, was forced to travel to London in order to be consecrated by a bishop, as was the requirement—in his case, the ceremony was performed by the Bishop of London.

Aaron's son, yet another Aaron, became a Congregationalist minister and, as a member of the Connecticut state legislature, introduced the first bill in American history calling for the abolition of slavery.

A forebear, a Moses Cleaveland too, after distinguished military service in the American Revolution, was a successful lawyer in Canterbury, Connecticut, and served in the state convention that ratified the Constitution in 1788. In 1795 he led a group of investors who participated in the Connecticut Land Company's purchase of three million acres of Connecticut's Western Reserve. He and a party of associates in the following year established a settlement on the south shore of Lake Erie at the mouth of the Cuyahoga River. Named Cleaveland, in salute to Moses's efforts, the little village, which had become a thriving town by the time Grover was born, finally dropped the "a" in 1832, when, it was reported, the local newspaper had need to shorten its masthead.

Young Grover was conscious that his people were patriots whose deeds were tied to the history of the country. He knew much about the national heroes. When he was only nine years old, in writing a composition on the value of industriousness, he pointed out: "George Washington improved his time when he was a boy and he was not sorry when he was at the head of a large army fighting for his country. . . . Jackson was a poor boy but he was placed in school and by improving his time he found himself president of the United States guiding and directing a powerful nation."

During Grover's growing up, public services were nonexistent and not expected. While Philadelphia had provided itself with a water system in 1801, and New York followed suit a generation later, small communities like Fayetteville relied on local waterways and wells. Although uniformed police came into being in the 1850s, the Fayettevilles of America did not have them until the beginning of the twentieth century. Fire was the great scourge of every community; the only fighters were volunteers who were ill-equipped and almost invariably too late on the scene. Except for New York City's pioneering omnibus running on Broadway, there was no public transportation.

Most people knew that the code for intimate relationships was strict, and prudery—at least in public—was universal. Not until after the Civil War did newspapers carry sometimes titillating advertisements for nostrums to cure sexual ailments. Professional and spectator sports—except for horse racing—were still in the future. Intellectual life was for the few because the physical labor of conquering the land was still the country's chief business. Indeed, "culture" was regarded as decidedly feminine; and, in general, "masculinity" was expected to distinguish itself by a lack of exterior polish. It is not apparent that Grover Cleveland defied this convention.

The boy Cleveland received the usual strict training. The day of the child-centered home had not yet dawned. Children were expected to be little adults, disciplined and responsible for their behavior, and chastised promptly for misperforming. In the Cleveland home, the parents' wishes and words were received as commands. Cleveland would later say: "Often and often as a boy, I was compelled to get out of my warm bed at night, to hang up a hat or other garment which I had left on the floor." There were no luxuries to embellish or soften life, for the parents, raising nine children, had no income other than the minister's salary, which for many years never exceeded $600 a year. Still, the family had a servant, a Canadian woman, who helped in preparing meals. Grover, like his brothers and sisters, was sometimes enlisted to take care of the younger ones, often having to sacrifice playtime with friends. In the muscular Christianity in which the children were reared, they all understood that Sunday was a day for Sunday school, worship, and, as ordained in the Bible, surcease from work. For the father it meant he must deliver two sermons, in addition to performing other sacerdotal duties. For the mother it was a time to rest from her burden of doing the mercy tasks of the pastorate.

Richard Cleveland served in Fayetteville for nine years. Never robust, his health began to decline, and he was glad to accept a less demanding place with the American Home Missionary Society in Clinton, New York, which carried an annual salary of one thousand dollars. The move to Clinton in 1851 was a harsh blow to Grover, then fourteen years old. Adolescents find uprooting hard, and Grover was no exception. Perhaps he was resentful and maybe even tearful. There was no way for him to keep in touch with his old friends, for letter writing was not the style among boys on the verge of manhood. Cleveland always recalled his time in Fayetteville as the best days of his youth. Even when as president he visited the town, he spoke with deep emotion of the benefits he had received there: "They have gone with me in every step in life."

The family remained in Clinton for three years. Grover was eager to prepare himself for Hamilton College, conveniently situated in the town, and the school from which his brother William was almost ready to graduate. Grover was not a natural linguist, and he never forgot the difficulties he had had in learning Latin in the Clinton academy he attended. Still, this deficiency was not what prevented him from going to college: his impoverished family required that he get a job. He returned to Fayetteville to work as a clerk in the village store. The salary was fifty dollars for the first year and one hundred dollars for the second, lodging and meals included. The husky young man rose each morning at five o'clock in an unheated, unadorned room he shared with a fellow clerk, and began his monotonous chore for long hours.

After two years, he returned to Clinton with high hopes of now beginning his college education. But fate again intervened. His father, still in delicate health, found even his position in Clinton too demanding, and he opted in 1853 to take a rural pastorate in Holland Patent, a small village fifteen miles north of Utica. Three weeks after entering upon his new ministry, he died, leaving a widow and children destitute. Grover's immediate future was now fixed: he would have to help in the family's support. His dream of attending Hamilton College was shattered. Years later during his presidency, speaking at Harvard's

250th anniversary, he revealed, as emotionally as he dared in public, that he was but an "invited guest" and that "the reflection that for me there is no alma mater, gives rise to a feeling of regret."

Grover's elder brother, William, was a teacher at the New York Institution for the Blind in New York City. Diligent like Grover, William was promoted to principal and quickly hired Grover as his assistant. The work was demanding and required infinite patience. Grover had sympathy as well as patience, but he knew that a career in this occupation was not for him. After a year at the institution, he was now determined to study law. He went home to his mother. She had continued to live in Holland Patent and would do so until her death in 1882. Grover's youngest sister, Rose Elizabeth—always "Libbie" to him and he always "Grove" to her—who published essays on notable literary women, also made her home there.

A family neighbor, Ingham Townsend, a wealthy Presbyterian elder of Holland Patent who admired Grover for his reliability and steadiness, offered to help him go to college in order to enter the ministry. Grover possibly had thought of following in his father's footsteps, but perhaps his experience in New York City had opened his mind to the larger world of affairs. The kindly Townsend yielded to Grover's request to lend him twenty-five dollars so that the young man could travel to Cleveland, Ohio, in order to undertake the study of law. Twelve years later Cleveland would repay the loan with interest, reminding Townsend that the "loan you made me was my start in life."

On his way west, Grover decided to stop off in Buffalo to visit his uncle, Lewis W. Allen, whose home in Black Rock, a community recently annexed to Buffalo, he had often visited during his boyhood. Allen was a wealthy farmer with a herd of shorthorn cattle. What Grover expected to be a brief stopover proved to be the opposite, and a major turning point. Uncle Lewis, hearing from Grover that he planned to go to Cleveland to study law, insisted that Buffalo was where he ought to put down his roots. Being well-connected and well-liked, Allen was in a position to help him get started. He offered him not only bed and board but a salary for helping him finish the little book he was writing: the *Short-horn Herd Book*.

With the advantage of Allen's introduction, Grover entered the law firm of Rogers, Bowen, and Rogers, whose senior partner, Henry W. Rogers, knew everybody in town. Cleveland was well aware that he was in President Fillmore's old firm—which remains the only company of lawyers able to boast that two of its number went forth from its office on a road to the White House. Whatever dreams were animating the young aspirant, for now, in the time-honored fashion, he would read legal tomes, especially Blackstone, and observe the law as practiced, and eventually when his elders deemed him ready, he would be admitted to the bar. Grover Cleveland's life was beginning afresh in Buffalo.

2

A Career in Buffalo

The Buffalo that Cleveland was making his home in was a well-off and bustling lake city of a hundred thousand. The population had doubled in the previous ten years. Incorporated in 1832, a year before Chicago, it was, like Chicago, a Great Lakes commercial center competing with the Windy City in size and vigor. The Buffalonians felt all the moods and tumults of the country at large. The Michigan Street Baptist Church, for instance, is remembered even today for being a way station on the Underground Railroad, the last stop on the path to Canada and freedom for fugitive slaves. And the city was proud to recollect that in 1835 when a fleeing slave family that had recently escaped to Canada was kidnapped from St. Catherine's in Ontario and brought to Buffalo, blacks liberated the victims and returned them across the border.

Even so, the slavery issue was not an element in Buffalo politics. It was the economic growth of the city that riveted the attention and energy of the populace. The docks were crowded with lake vessels bringing grain on its way to England and from there to the continent of Europe. All that held back growth was a shortage of manual labor. In 1842 the town had the first steam-powered grain elevator in the United States to help alleviate that lack. Buffalo was also a stopping-off place for people on their way to Chicago. In only five days a traveler from New York or Boston could journey to Chicago by taking a train to Buffalo and then boarding such a vessel as the luxurious lake boat *Hendrik Hudson* for the second leg of the trip. Shipbuilding was a considerable source of jobs, and many of the best and best-known of the lake boats came down the ways in Buffalo.

Buffalo's economic activity had already persuaded the population to think of itself as a living dynamo. In 1844 the city had been linked by railroad to Albany, New York, providing new opportunities for mutual trade. The physical expansion of the city from four and a half square miles to forty-two in 1854 opened the door to new possibilities for big-city activities. The growth had come from the influx of Germans, some fleeing the unrest or oppression in their homeland, and Irish people salvaged from the great potato famine of 1846 that took so many lives of their countrymen. The population included about seven hundred blacks.

Political interest centered on local matters and for a long time around the president of the United States, a native Buffalonian who, only two years before Grover Cleveland arrived on the scene, had returned to his home there. Millard Fillmore, a Whig, was elected vice president in 1848, and became president upon the death of Zachary Taylor in 1850. His rise from the State Assembly to the House of Representatives had fascinated his fellow citizens. His role as president in helping make possible the Compromise of 1850 had brought fresh pride to his hometown. The sentiment for the Union was strong, because any disruption of it meant a disruption of the lifelines of commerce.

Nevertheless, when Fillmore aimed to become president in his own right by running in 1856 on the anti-Catholic and anti-immigrant party, the Know-Nothings, he astonished and offended hordes of former supporters and admirers. To the Roman Catholics—Irish and German—who were flocking into the city, the Know-Nothings were anathema. Pope Pius IX gave Buffalo its first Roman Catholic bishop—John Timon of Pennsylvania in

1854—evidence of the growing strength of the denomination. Bishop Timon had proceeded to build a cathedral on the main street, between the two oldest Protestant churches.

The German and Irish immigrants, constituting about 60 percent of Buffalo's population, had brought with them from the old country their love of beer. For workingmen who slaved long hours and often seven days a week, alcohol was the sure anodyne. Some Buffalonians liked to joke that Buffalo had a "bar on every corner." There was a tavern, it was said, for every eighty-four residents. The truth was not so comprehensive. The city in 1872 had thirty-five breweries—not an unusually large number for a municipality so large. The principal brewer was Gerhard Lang, who, like his competitors, opened saloons as places where his product was served exclusively. At one time, Lang owned eighty outlets. Many of those not owned by Lang were what we would call "microbreweries." Practically every evening, thirsty patrons could be seen on their way to their favorite saloon, each man swinging on its wire handle a pint can that the Germans nicknamed their *Grallers* or grails. The taverns that drew such a large part of the male population were not merely beer taps; they also did service as community centers and political meeting rooms.

In this heady environment, Cleveland, studious and attentive to detail, found contentment. His days of poverty and constant concern about his future seemed over. In the comfortable embrace of his uncle's affluent home, and in the company of the leading and most influential figures of Buffalo—many of whom he met at his law office—he enjoyed excellent prospects. Having been admitted to the bar in 1859, he remained at his desk where, as student and clerk, he was daily proving his worth to the partners. When he left the firm in 1862, the Civil War was about to reach its climax. Although he had seen Buffalo youths, many of them his friends, and many of them the sons of business acquaintances, march off to fight, Cleveland had not joined them. He legally avoided the military draft by obtaining a substitute, a thirty-two-year-old Polish immigrant, to take his place for $150—and who, it must be noted, survived the war.

Cleveland had come to be the chief support of his mother and sisters—and his contributions to their upkeep were becoming substantial. The Clevelands could be satisfied that they were suitably represented in the struggle to save the Union: two younger sons were in the Union army. Grover was proud of their service, but whether he envied them their place we do not know. A few years after the war's end, both young men lost their lives at sea in the burning of the steamship *Missouri*—tragic deaths that left the family inconsolable and increased dependence on Grover more than ever.

Cleveland accepted appointment in January 1863 as assistant district attorney of Erie County. It is not clear whether he felt he must seek new opportunity, or whether he was drawn to public service because he felt pangs of guilt that he was not in a military uniform. In any case, the position gave him a broad and fresh view of public affairs. The district attorney, C. C. Torrance, quickly found Cleveland to be a glutton for work, and as he himself lived at a considerable distance from Buffalo, he found it convenient to allow his young assistant to perform the lion's share of the office's duties.

Cleveland made the most of the freedom his chief allowed him, soon becoming familiar with his opposite numbers in the other counties and making himself increasingly useful to businesspeople. A few years later, at the expiration of Torrance's term, the Democratic leaders nominated Cleveland, then only twenty-eight years old, to take over. This was Cleveland's first run for office—his first effort to try his skill as a politician. But the county was staunchly Republican, and Lyman K. Bass, only a few months older than Cleveland, and destined to serve two terms in the U.S. House of Representatives, defeated Cleveland in a close election. Unfazed by defeat, Cleveland did the next best thing: he formed his own law firm, in partnership with Isaac K. Vanderpoel. The association lasted only briefly because Vanderpoel departed to become a police magistrate.

In 1869, Cleveland and two other up-and-coming lawyers, Oscar Folsom and Albert P. Laning, joined together to establish

Laning, Cleveland, and Folsom. It prospered quickly. While Cleveland was the workhorse, Laning, a corporate attorney in the first generation of that breed, was the "rainmaker," bringing in the legal business of the New York Central and other railroads. Folsom, a charming, happy-go-lucky fellow—as well as an able attorney—made friends wherever he went and helped give the firm a public face. He complemented perfectly Cleveland's somewhat rigid conventionality, and the two men were drawn to each other in mutual affection like iron filings to a magnet.

But once again, public service lured Cleveland. In the fall of 1870 he decided to accept the nomination of sheriff for the county, and he easily won the position. It is hard to see why Cleveland, now an experienced and accomplished lawyer, known for the thoroughness with which he prepared his cases and for his apparent affection for the law, should seek this office. Many of its duties were distasteful, for they included serving warrants and dispossess notices on delinquent renters. Still, there was less pressure in the post than he could see was becoming his daily lot, and the healthy fees that sheriffs earned were attractive. Moreover, he looked forward to more leisure time than he had enjoyed since he was a boy.

As sheriff, he refused to pass on to others the unpleasant responsibilities that befell his office, and several times as prisoners stood on the gallows, he himself pulled the lever sending them to their death. Later, political foes would take devilish pleasure in referring to him as the Buffalo Hangman. Still, by all accounts, his term in the sheriff's office served him well: he had been able to save a good portion of his salary; he had consolidated his connections with almost every segment of officialdom; and his diligence had made a strong impression on people throughout his constituency. He was a public personage, appreciated and respected.

Cleveland, as he had been from his youth, remained a straight arrow. He was shy with women, and he made intimate friends only slowly. Still, although a bachelor, he was not a loner. The saloons of Buffalo were his social halls, and his increasing girth left no doubt that he enjoyed what they served. Almost from the time he had arrived in town, he had been a tavern patron, but never a boozer. He was surely "one of the boys," but he maintained the dignity that had been bred into him. In that age before dress-down and leisure garb, he could be spotted in white shirt and tie speaking atop an upended barrel about the issues of the day to an appreciative crowd. For many of the immigrants, who read no English, there were few sources of information. A man like Cleveland, holding forth clearly in simple words, was a pipeline to knowledge they wanted and, in his way, a helper in their Americanization. The bars of the city were noisy with the clamor of relaxed workingmen, and the sound of a politician quieting his audience as he stood up to talk could be a welcome relief from the usual din.

After his term as sheriff ended, Cleveland was back in private practice, his old firm having continued on its own. He created a partnership with Wilson Shannon Bissell, known to intimates as "Shan," and his old foe, Lyman Bass, now serving in Congress. Bissell, a Yale alumnus, was a popular man at the law firm where Cleveland had his first job. More than ten years younger than Cleveland, the two had gradually become inseparable companions, and they could be seen on many a night at the watering holes they patronized for recreation. Bass, plagued since childhood by ill health, soon left for Colorado Springs in the hope of recovering, and George J. Sicard replaced him as a name partner. The firm was now Cleveland, Bissell & Sicard. It would be Cleveland's final foray in the private sector, and it prospered almost immediately. Cleveland was an excellent litigator, and judges and fellow lawyers, not to speak of clients, admired especially the fastidiousness of his preparation for court appearances, his briefs being a model of detail and lucidity. The fees for his services rose steadily, and it is no exaggeration to say that he had become a moderately well-to-do man. Some of his income came from referee fees that his good friends in the courts sent his way.

Cleveland's upbringing, however, had accustomed him to living within his means, and never to forget that a rainy day could occur. Had Cleveland remained a counselor-at-law catering to the booming business community, his biography would have become a rags-to-riches story in the best tradition of the century. But the excitement of politics and the ideal of public service remained irresistible lures. He always risked much when he yielded to the temptation of running for office, having done so now for a second time. He would later say, "This office-seeking is a disease. It is even catching."

The dominating figure in Buffalo politics was Joseph Warren, the owner of the *Courier*, the city's leading newspaper. Like many another New Englander who had migrated westward in the "Yankee exodus" that was depeopling places like his native Vermont, Warren was an energetic leader of the Democratic Party. A community-minded and magnetic force in Buffalo affairs, he did not hanker after political office for himself. Instead, he constantly had an eye out for other men who shared his spirit of boosterism. Grover Cleveland, who had become a good friend of his, was one of them.

When Warren died in 1876, Cleveland could have taken over the leadership of the party in Erie County, but his extensive law practice did not allow the commitment of time the role entailed. Still, he served on party committees and kept in close touch with the ebb and flow of political tides. Through the close presidential election in 1880 that brought a narrow victory to the Republican James A. Garfield, the Democratic Party, long stigmatized as the "party of the rebellion," showed revived strength. In New York, Garfield had received only twenty-one thousand more votes than the Democrat, Winfield Scott Hancock.

In 1881, the Democratic Party in Buffalo, looking for a mayor who could command widespread respect and undertake the municipal reform that was becoming now the watchword of striving office seekers, turned to Cleveland as its first choice. The city government—like many in the nation coping with pressing urban problems in the aftermath of the Civil War—was in the hands of a notoriously corrupt bipartisan ring. Cleveland demurred at first, whether out of feigned modesty or genuine reluctance, it is impossible to say. He had just turned down an offer from the New York Central Railroad to become its general counsel for western New York. The mayoralty carried an annual salary of only $2,500. Being unmarried, Cleveland could afford to take the office, and he was lured by the challenge. In a lively campaign, his passion for reform rang out in the numberless speeches he delivered in the back rooms of the waterfront taverns where he felt so much at home. His opponents found it hard to make a case against his candidacy, although one detractor said that Cleveland was prejudiced against married people. His supporters rejoined: "He is a jovial, genial companion, and probably delights in association with his own sex." On Election Day, he won by a majority of thirty-five hundred over the opposition. Thus it came about that on the first day of January in 1882, Cleveland was mayor of Buffalo.

That his would be a new kind of governance he foreshadowed in his acceptance address. He stated in unaffected language that a city ought to be able to conduct its affairs with the same efficiency and effectiveness as a private business. It did not seem right or logical, he pointed out, that the paving, lighting, and cleaning of the streets should depend on the party affiliation of the working people. In short order, he put his conviction into practice, exposing a plot to overcharge the city $100,000 on a road-construction project. He showed Buffalo a novel kind of management when he supervised the building of a new sewage system without greasing any palms. His energy and intense devotion to duty and to the law were duly noticed. When a proposal was introduced to use five hundred dollars from the city's Fourth of July fund in order to celebrate the new Decoration Day holiday honoring the Civil War dead, Cleveland refused to permit such a shift of money. It would violate the public's intention, he maintained. It was not that he opposed the celebration of Decoration Day. Indeed, he put himself at the head of a group to raise funds to mark it. Old-time politicos were appalled at such a stickler for honesty, but the public as a whole was full of esteem and amazement.

Before that first year in office was out, a boomlet to make Cleveland the next governor of New York had begun. While he avowed that he was not in any way promoting such a candidacy, he did not dismiss the notion. In a letter to one of his first supporters he declared with characteristic obliqueness: "If it were not for my abiding faith in the success of an honest effort to perform public duty, I should at times distrust my ability to properly bear the responsibilities of the place in case of election." He was saying yes and offering his growing reputation for uprightness in office as his chief credential. "Good and pure government lies at the foundation of the wealth and progress of every community," was how he phrased his philosophy at a cornerstone-laying ceremony of the Young Men's Christian Association. This simple sentiment would become the mantra of his political career. His mother's pride in her son and in the way he was displaying what he had learned at her knee must have been immense. Still, she did not live to see what was yet to be. On July 19, 1882, in her seventy-eighth year, Ann Neal Cleveland died in Holland Patent, Grover at her bedside.

3

Governor of New York

The year 1882, which had seen the restarting of Cleveland's public career, witnessed also renewed and uncommon turmoil in the country's national political life. The assassination of President Garfield, who had lingered from July to September of the previous year, had, in a way, put a hold on national politics. And the accession of Chester A. Arthur had brought a third New Yorker to the White House. The reverberations were felt in Buffalo. The general knowledge that a disappointed office seeker was Garfield's slayer increased the clamor for civil-service reform.

Other forces, aside from an aroused electorate, were also at work for reform. In the years following the Civil War, demands on government had become more complex. Officials in the various bureaucracies required specialized—sometimes highly technical—knowledge, and their positions could not be filled adequately if the appointees' chief qualification was that they happened to know the right politician. Moreover, as urban government, in particular, grew larger, the turnover of key positions after every change of party could bring chaos to daily life, which cried out for continuity in public services. Cleveland, the politician of integrity, manifestly was riding with the wind of change at his back.

Corruption, which customarily meant bribery as well as out-
right theft of public funds, was rife in both major parties. The
dramatic revelations about the corrupt Tweed Ring in New York
City had tended to discredit all Democrats, but the corruption
of some Republican politicians upstate, who accepted cash and
favors from William Tweed and his henchmen, was not unnoticed. Besides, the Republican administration of General Grant
was being fixed in the public mind as the most corrupt presidency in the nation's history. It had not kept Grant in 1872 from
winning reelection, nor the Republican candidate for governor
of New York, John Adams Dix, from riding on Grant's coattails
and handily defeating Francis Kernan, the choice of the Democrats and Liberal Republicans. Nevertheless, even ordinary citizens were now sensitized to the shenanigans of so many of their
politicians, and there was a widespread feeling that corruption
was undermining the republic itself, and that it was time to
clean out the stables.

Governor Dix, scenting change in the air, had quickly taken
advantage of his party's favored position. He removed some of
the worst features of New York City's charter fashioned by
the Tweed machine. He abolished property qualifications for
black voters, gave governors the line-item veto of appropriation
bills, forbade certain extra payments to state contractors, and
increased the term of the governor from two to three years
(twenty years later it would be reduced to two again). At the
same time, Dix was unable to overthrow the spoils system, even
though we now can see that it was on its last legs. The richest
state in the Union required efficiency and probity in the management of its affairs.

The work of helping to bring that requirement about fell to
the Democrats, and Grover Cleveland played his part in it. But
beforehand, the stage belonged to Samuel J. Tilden. A drab,
secretive, and fragile man constantly said to be ailing, he was
called behind his back Simpering Sammy. Yet, despite all, he was
a determined voice for reform and a lawyer remarkably able to
marshal facts and figures persuasively. He had once been known

as the Great Forecloser because of his unsentimental style as a businessman; now he was called the Great Reformer. Although the *New York Times* deserves most of the credit for exposing the Tweed Ring, Tilden personified the challenger who called for clean municipal government. Already in 1868 his yeoman service for Horatio Seymour, the Democratic candidate for president and a fellow New Yorker, had given Tilden prominence throughout the party. So, despite his weak speaking voice and an unimposing, even off-putting presence, Tilden became a natural candidate for governor in 1874. He easily defeated the incumbent Dix by fifty thousand votes.

Though cautious and timid, Tilden in his time in Albany was a reformer's dream. He reduced taxes and completed the work of destroying the Tweed crowd. He also successfully prosecuted the Canal Ring, another notorious group of politicians and businessmen in cahoots to fleece the state by their overcharges for repairing and building waterways in the northern part of the state.

Cleveland watched all of this with his habitual attentiveness. He was not close to Tilden personally, no doubt because both he and the governor were intensely private in habit and slow to accept intimacy with others. Cleveland also made a virtue of the self-reliance he had learned at home as a boy, so he was not given to approaching others for help. Years later, Tilden was asked what sort of person he believed Cleveland to be, and he replied: "Oh, he is the kind of man who would rather do something badly for himself than to have somebody else do it well."

In 1876 Tilden, now a national figure, a symbol of good government in the nation's centennial year, was nominated for president at the Democratic convention in St. Louis. A mark of his strength was that he became the standard-bearer on the second ballot. The running mate chosen to balance the ticket was Thomas A. Hendricks of Ohio, a soft-money man, which in those days meant a supporter of cheap paper currency. Meanwhile, back in New York, Tilden's successor in Albany was his lieutenant governor, Lucius Robinson. Robinson, now sixty-seven

years old, was a party hack. Pledged to continue Tilden's pro-
gram of reform, he was hamstrung by the hostility of Tammany
Hall, particularly the leadership there of "Honest" John Kelly,
Boss Tweed's successor in the club's wigwam.

In 1879 Robinson was defeated for reelection, becoming one
more one-termer on the roll of New York governors. He ran
poorly against Alonzo B. Cornell, an ally of the senior U.S. senator from New York, Roscoe Conkling. Cornell's serpentine road
to the governorship had been closely linked with Conkling's
influence in the state and his machinations in Washington.

Conkling, a leader of the Stalwart Republicans, had been a
familiar figure on Capitol Hill since 1858 when he arrived as
a member of the House of Representatives. In the "age of the
spoilsmen," as the time has been labeled, he was one of the king-
pins. He enforced an iron discipline on the party underlings,
even as he inspired them with his jingoistic oratory. He strutted
like a peacock, often attired in white flannel trousers, bright-
colored vests, and jackets adorned with lace cuffs. And in words
that became famous, he had trumpeted: "Parties are not built up
by deportment, or by ladies' magazines, or gush." Parties would
die, he predicted, if the faithful could not be rewarded with
jobs. In party matters, the voice of the party spokesman had the
force of law.

Cornell, the Conkling acolyte, was the son of Ezra Cornell,
founder of Cornell University and tycoon of the Western Electric Telegraph Company. Ezra Cornell had been speaker of the
New York assembly and an ally of Conkling. President Grant,
bowing to Conkling's power, had appointed Alonzo Cornell to
the lucrative office of naval officer of the New York custom
house. When President Rutherford B. Hayes, Grant's successor,
issued an executive order declaring that federal officeholders
were forbidden to engage in party management, Cornell, out-
raged, refused to yield his party position. Thereupon, Hayes sus-
pended him.

The New York Republican organization promptly defied the
White House by nominating Cornell to be governor of New

York. Cornell, to the dismay of his old associates, changed his stripes and decided to plump for clean government. The Conkling forces became suspicious, as well as simply furious. They concluded that Cornell was trying to build his own machine. But the man stuck to his guns and performed without scandal. He expected to be renominated and reelected. The party, though, would have none of it. He had betrayed Conkling, onetime friend and fellow operative in skulduggery, who soon came to loathe him and refer to him as "that lizard on the hill."

Continuing to battle the White House, whoever occupied it, Conkling went to war against President Garfield, despite the fact that Chester A. Arthur, a henchman of Conkling's in New York, was the vice president. Garfield, in his brief time in office, had bluntly rebuffed Conkling's claim to control the spoils of office in New York and ignored the senator in making an appointment to the New York custom house.

Conkling, deeply wounded, responded almost instantaneously. He resigned from the Senate and persuaded his close associate, the other New York senator, Tom Platt, to do likewise. Platt would ever after be known as "Me, Too" Platt. They confidently expected to be reelected by the usually pliant New York legislature, then the electors of the Senate. If returned to Washington, the pair could thumb their noses at the president. Before that sweet revenge, alas, Garfield died, and Arthur was president. The angry ex-senators were hoist by their own petard: erstwhile friends in Albany denied them their ticket back to Washington. And Cornell gave no help to his old buddy Conkling.

The Democratic Party was about to be the beneficiary of this earthquake rumbling beneath the Republican turf. The canvass for governor in 1882 was a testing time in American politics although at the moment few were aware fully of its significance. The conventions of the parties were set for the week of September 17, the Democrats were going to meet in Syracuse and the Republicans in Saratoga. The guiding spirit of the Republicans was Jay Gould, once an ally of Boss Tweed, and a man whose name, it was said, was spoken by decent people only after sprinkling disinfectant. Cornell deserved to be nominated on the basis of the good work he had done in pressing for reform. He had earned plaudits and the backing of many new members of the legislature, including young Theodore Roosevelt, an up-and-coming politician, just two years out of Harvard.

But Cornell was a gone goose. Enough of the old spoilsmen were still around. They nominated Charles J. Folger, a decent man personally, who was chief judge of the Court of Appeals. He had turned down Garfield's offer of the post of attorney general, but soon afterward accepted appointment as secretary of the Treasury. No one questioned his experience or his uprightness. He was tainted, however, by the support of Conkling and Gould, and of Arthur, whose recent conversion to reform was deemed by many people to be insincere. It was widely believed that Gould's presence in Saratoga meant that his lucre was available to obtain the nomination for Folger by bribing Cornell's delegates to desert him. In the event, Folger defeated Cornell in the convention 257 to 222.

In the months before the Democrats assembled, many people in the state thought that the outstanding candidates were Roswell P. Flower and the hero-general Henry W. Slocum. Flower, born in humble circumstances and fatherless while still a boy, had married well. Through his wife, he became a power on Wall Street and an immensely rich man. His word, it was said, was "worth a million dollars at any time." He became a major player in the Democratic Party and in 1881, when President Garfield sent Levi P. Morton to Paris as the U.S. Minister to France, Flower ran for and won Morton's seat in the House of Representatives. Like others of his day he was prepared to leave Washington to become chief executive in his home state.

As for General Slocum, he was an illustrious name since the Civil War for his gallant service from First Bull Run on to Chancellorsville, Chickamauga, Gettysburg, and finally in Sherman's march through Georgia. Trained as a lawyer, as well as a professional soldier (he had been graduated from West Point in 1852), he was easily elected to a seat in the House of Representatives in 1868 and then for a second term. After serving as commissioner of public works in Brooklyn, he was returned to Congress in 1882. His claim to be the next governor seemed unassailable.

Grover Cleveland, though, with a much less glamorous record, still relatively untested, and a novice in rich-stake politics, was on the minds of some of the leaders of the party. He loomed as a "new man," like those ancient Roman citizens who could obtain high places without the background of family or military accomplishment. A local favorite, who as mayoral candidate had attracted the support of "the better class," his record in office had strengthened and enlarged his following. But he was hardly known outside the state, as Flower and Slocum were.

The Democratic kingmaker was Daniel Manning. Like Flower, he had risen from an impoverished family to be a substantial presence in politics. A journalist of considerable talent, during the Civil War he was legislative correspondent of the *Brooklyn Eagle*. Subsequently he worked at the *Albany Argus*, covering the state senate. In time he became president of the paper, the most influential sheet in the capital. As a close friend and political lieutenant of Samuel J. Tilden, he succeeded him as the effective head of the New York State Democratic Party after the election of 1876, and served as actual chairman from 1881 to 1885.

Manning was a low-key, thoughtful person, who did not seek public office himself. But his wisdom and influence was sought by others who were ambitious of office. Cleveland, able to drop his law practice for a meager-paying public post, appealed to Manning, who was constantly on the lookout for good candidates. Besides, Cleveland had the merit of having incensed Tammany by some of his actions as mayor, which gave him a shining reputation for the battle against the spoils system. In a notable move, Cleveland had adamantly opposed the reelection of Tammany's man, Thomas F. Grady, to be the leader of the State Senate. As a result, John Kelly, long wary of Cleveland, came to regard him as Tammany's enemy number one—a label that Cleveland would wear with pride.

Meanwhile, Cleveland played the bashful coquette. For example, he wrote to Edgar K. Apgar, the young deputy secretary of state and deputy treasurer of the party, who was the first to throw Cleveland's hat into the ring: "I know that neither my acquaintance in political circles, nor my standing in the State Democracy, would for a moment suggest my name as a proper one to head the ticket in the coming campaign. And if it were not for my abiding faith in the success of an honest effort to perform public duty, I should at times distrust my ability to properly bear the responsibilities of the place in case of election." Dan Manning, though, was convinced that Cleveland was the man. It proved to be the case.

Soon it became clear that the able and somewhat diffident Folger had only lukewarm support from the newspapers that counted: the *Albany Journal*, the *New York Times*, and the *New York Tribune*. The coffers of the party were empty, and the friends of the old trio, Conkling, Arthur, and Garfield, had no enthusiasm for his reelection. On November 7, 1882, Grover Cleveland was elected by a majority of 192,000 votes, the largest margin ever registered in a contested election for the highest office in the state. The tally is impressive:

Grover Cleveland, Democrat	535,318
Charles J. Folger, Republican	342,464
Alphonse A. Hopkins, Prohibition	25,783
Epenetus Howe, Greenback	11,974
blank and miscellaneous	3,335

Moreover, it was a Democratic sweep as the party picked up twenty-one seats in the House of Representatives and won a large majority in the state assembly.

Cleveland looked confident on the night of the election, but he had anxiety too. He had never been afraid of facing the unknown, yet the burden of responsibility had always weighed heavily upon him. On Election Day he had written to his brother William, now a clergyman in Buffalo, a surrogate for their mother, only recently deceased, to whom Grover lamented he would have preferred to be writing. I shall serve, he stated, with "no idea of reelection, or any higher political preferment in my head, but be very thankful and happy if I can well serve one term as the people's Governor." And, he added, "Do you know that if mother were alive, I should feel so much safer? I have always thought that her prayers had much to do with my success."

The Democratic victory was so stunning that it became the theme of the popular vaudeville team of Harrigan and Hart. They sang a ditty with an Irish brogue at a time when mocking immigrant accents was acceptable in vaudeville theater. The reference to the "army" echoed the common advice to dullards and other tiresome people: "Go join the Salvation Army":

> *Cleveland and Folger, they had a fight;*
> *Cleveland hit Folger with all his might.*
> *The winner lives in Buffalo,*
> *The loser will jine the a-a-army-o.*

The audience took up the chorus again and again as they tried to outsing Harrigan and Hart:

> *Away, away, away we go,*
> *Away, away, away we go,*
> *Away, away, away we go,*
> *To jine the Salvation A-a-army-o.*

Cleveland prepared for the executive mansion with his habitual calm attention to detail, treating the next step in his career as if it were an ordinary, expected occurrence. Even as he was resigning as mayor, his name was being mentioned for the presidency: The *New York Tribune* was saying that the next nominee of the Democrats would have to be either Cleveland or Benjamin Butler, the governor of Massachusetts. On December 6 a reception in honor of Cleveland was held at the Manhattan Club in

New York City. Democrats from all the neighboring states were in attendance—except Butler, who was sulking in Massachusetts and had forbidden any of his cronies to be in the city saluting the new governor there. As long ago as 1862 when he was a Republican, Butler had been lusting after the presidency; Cleveland seemed to him only the latest impediment to his goal.

Cleveland, in his address before his peers, knowing he was being "looked over," uttered not very original words, simply ones that winners invariably find handy: the election was a triumph of the people, and it was the victor's obligation and wish to fulfill their high expectations. Still, Cleveland was mindful also of the changed weather covering the political landscape: "We shall utterly fail to read aright the signs of the times if we are not fully convinced that parties are but the instruments through which the public work their will. . . . The vanquished have lately learned these things, and the victors will act wisely if they profit by the lesson."

The new governor prepared his inaugural address with the expectation that his role was to be a unifier. And the administration would be a youthful one. Cleveland, not yet forty-six years old, had, at Manning's urging, selected Daniel Lamont, a thirty-two-year-old staff member of the *Argus*, to be his private and military secretary. Lamont, who, as a dropout from Union College in Schenectady, New York, had become a protégé of Samuel Tilden, was endowed with a winning manner and shrewd political instincts. He quickly became Cleveland's chief political adviser and factotum, and during the next fifteen years was a major force in Cleveland's life. It became well known to newspaper reporters that to get action on an idea or a bill it was necessary to "see Lamont." The governor-elect informed Lamont on the day after Christmas that the inaugural speech was complete and that it was being copied by a stenographer who would run it through "a printing machine"—one of the newfangled devices called typewriters now coming into general use.

Although Cleveland had written his brother that he did not intend to seek higher office, it is impossible to believe that the idea of running for president had failed to cross his mind. Meanwhile, the task in hand was formidable. He confronted the burden of occupying the executive mansion in Albany. Being still a single man, he may have wished to have a wife, but there is no evidence that he ever talked or wrote of himself as being lonely. As he contemplated living in the cavernous official residence, he considered asking his sister Rose to join him there to supervise the housekeeping. Since he did not intend to do any formal entertaining, he decided he did not require a hostess. He invited the chief steward at the City Club, William Sinclair, a light-skinned black man, to join him as a personal aide. Sinclair, flattered by the offer, declined it but instead suggested that Cleveland take his son, also William, who promptly was pleased to have the opportunity and headed for Albany to prepare for Cleveland's arrival.

On New Year's Eve, the governor-to-be, unannounced and accompanied only by "Shan" Bissell, who, with Manning, had managed the three-week campaign that had brought Cleveland to this magic moment, entered the mansion for the first time. Cleveland accepted the furnishings of his quarters as he found them. Nothing in his background had led him to think of decorating them afresh. His effects were few, and on the bureau he laid a Bible, its flyleaf inscribed simply: "My son, Stephen Grover Cleveland, from his loving Mother," a gift that he cherished deeply and that would follow him throughout his career. The book served, perhaps, as a way of having his mother present in spirit as he embarked on his august new public office.

On New Year's Day, with Bissell and Lamont on either side of him, he trudged through fresh-fallen snow to the State Capitol to take the oath of office in the assembly chamber. The inclement weather had forced the cancellation of the traditional military and civic parade, which resulted in an uncommonly meager ceremony, and sense of pomp and power.

A hush fell as Cleveland took the oath on his treasured Bible and began his address—delivered without notes. The spare, direct sentences he uttered were not inspiring. At the speaker's rostrum he had always been, as he was now, unsmiling and formal. His hearers did not expect a flight of oratory, and they did not get one. Although it was ordinary language that Cleveland spoke ("The interests now transferred to new hands are yours; and the duties here newly assumed should be performed for your benefit and your good."), these were not mere words of lip service. Cleveland had always behaved as if he were a man with a mission, and this fresh opportunity would not be for him anything less. So when he asked at the end of the brief address "for the forbearance of a just people, which I trust, will recognize a patriotic endeavor," he was speaking from the heart.

The next day he delivered his first message to the New York legislature. It did not bring good news to wealthy New Yorkers, for Cleveland made his chief point the unfairness of a tax system that laid levies on land and other real estate but not on personal property. The inequality of the arrangement, he pointed out, did not take into account that *all* property merited and required the protection of the state. To this call for an income tax the governor added his insistence that "all unnecessary offices should be abolished, and all employment of doubtful benefit discontinued." Thus, he would stand for fair taxation and smaller government. Smaller government presumably would strike a blow at the spoils system—a system now under fire throughout the country.

Because the phrase "civil service reform" was being heard everywhere, Cleveland was surfing on a wave of popular support. The leading voices in the movement were two magazine editors—George W. Curtis of *Harper's Weekly* and E. L. Godkin of *The Nation*. Many leaders in the civil service reform movement, who now brought their intensity to this new crusade, were men and women who had earlier been active in the abolitionist crusade and then had worked to secure civil rights for the recently freed slaves.

It must be observed that local political machines believed they played an indispensable role in the emerging industrial society that did not provide a "safety net" for people victimized by unemployment. The "boss" was the man who would send a holiday basket of food to a poor family, or get a youthful offender out of jail, or find a hospital bed for an injured worker. In an era of unbridled capitalism, the varied needs of a vast segment of the population were not met by charitable organizations, nor out of public funds. But although Cleveland deplored the "boss" system, he proposed no alternative arrangement to provide social security for the masses.

Not everyone took Cleveland's words to the legislature as a blueprint for action. Most of his hearers were simply sizing him up, aiming to prophesy the future by judging his comportment and presence, and imagining him in the legislative battles to come. What those struggles might be was forecast that very evening when Republican members of the assembly gathered their forces and in a portentous gesture—although futile because the Democrats controlled the body—elected Theodore Roosevelt as their minority leader.

The Democrats, more united than for many years in the past, were already looking forward to the presidential election of 1884. A generation of voters had grown up since the Civil War. The bloody shirt was no longer a useful banner to the Republicans. The G.A.R.—the Grand Army of the Republic, the powerful organization of Union army veterans once a veritable arm of the Republican Party—was growing thinner and less potent as new issues arose in the reunited states. No real Democrat had sat in the White House since James Buchanan left it in 1861, and the public had begun to assume that the presidency was "naturally" Republican. But when Tilden won the popular vote in 1876, and the formal end of Reconstruction came the following year, many voters began to think differently. The governorship of New York was regarded as second in importance only to the presidency itself, because of the state's central location, its growing population, and its economic primacy.

The rise of New York's port had been a major development for the whole country, and the Erie Canal had welded the Midwest to the Empire State. But even before then, New York was increasingly on the minds of those who ran the Democratic Party and looked to place its men in Washington. Between Jefferson's election in 1801 and the end of James Monroe's term in 1825, five of the six men who occupied the vice presidency had been New Yorkers, two of them former governors, George Clinton and Daniel Tompkins. Martin Van Buren's accession to the White House in 1837 broke fresh ground—the first president from the Empire State. In that era, the quality of leading New Yorkers had made a number of them national figures, although not presidents, including particularly Silas Wright, an unreconstructed Jacksonian; Thurlow Weed, a leading Whig; and William H. Seward, Lincoln's secretary of state. In 1868 and again in 1876, as we have seen, the Democratic Party nominees were former New York governors, Horatio Seymour and Samuel J. Tilden. Seymour was unable to defeat the great hero of the Union, Ulysses S. Grant, but Tilden had a quarter of a million more popular votes than Rutherford B. Hayes, who won in the electoral college.

Now Grover Cleveland was in the spotlight. He had captured the governorship of the largest state in the country after having served only a year as a mayor. He was far enough past the constitutionally required age of thirty-five to give confidence that he was not a tyro, and yet young enough to appeal to the new generation looking forward to managing the America of the Gilded Age.

Cleveland, moreover, had the advantage in the freshening atmosphere of politics of not having held a position in the legislature that produced political debts and other obligations. He had made his reputation, in large part, in fighting the sordid elements in his party. In a word, he would be benefited, not handcuffed, by his past in making the difficult judgments and recommendations his office required. His habits as a lawyer, notably a result of his training at home, had carried over into his public career. His legal briefs had been fashioned with impeccable care, his arguments measured and precise. Similarly, he did not speak words in his political utterances that he had not weighed and considered first in his mind and practiced in his thoughts. Winging it in public speech had not been Grover Cleveland's style up to now. Nor would it be his way as governor.

This undramatic style did not mask a forcefulness of spirit underneath. It was simply the reality of the man. It had its cost. Independence of the bosses was a good poster for a rising politician, but could it enact legislative initiatives? Cleveland soon found out. The boldness, the aggressiveness, of previous governors, Cleveland failed to show in that first message to the New York legislature. People knew that, in advocating an income tax, Cleveland was not treading new ground: there was a call for such a tax in many parts of the country. He did not get the change in taxation he was advocating—and had not expected to—but he had placed himself on the side of innovation.

While the inaugural address had been something of a failure, Cleveland soon took the reins of office firmly in hand. Before he had been in office two months, he sent the legislature eight veto messages, earning himself a new title: the Veto Governor. It has to be said, however, that the sponsors of the bills had introduced them knowing they would be vetoed, for all of them carried the odor of the pork barrel. Cleveland said no to Chautauqua County, which had proposed to spend money for a soldiers' monument. He said no to the Fredonia Library Association, which sought to be relieved of paying local taxes. He said no to the town of Elmira, which tried to avoid liability for personal injuries incurred by those traveling its unsafe streets and roads. Nor did sentiment sway him: he turned down the bid of Fayetteville, his boyhood hometown, to borrow money for the purchase of a new steam fire engine. In short, Cleveland, no skinflint, was merely keeping to his promise that he would be a guardian of the people's interests—which meant guarding the keys to the strongbox.

Still, Cleveland was not unfriendly to concerns beyond the small towns he was disciplining. With considerable courage he vetoed a bill to set a uniform rate of five cents for travel on the new elevated railroads in New York City. The varying and seemingly arbitrary high fares had both baffled and angered the passengers who had no option but to pay them. Bucking public opinion, Cleveland maintained that the proposed law was arbitrary and badly drawn. Moreover, he regarded the proposal as violating the charters of the railroads. Urged to allow the bill to become law without his signature, he scoffed at the thought. "I am convinced," he declared, "that in all cases the share which falls upon the Executive regarding the legislation of the State, should be in no manner evaded, but fairly met by the expression of his carefully guarded and unbiased judgment." If there had been a public opinion poll, the result likely might not have been favorable to the new governor, for a five-cent fare had many supporters—even among those who did not follow politics closely. The firmness of his stand, and his explanation of it, however, increased the high regard thousands had already felt for his career up to that point.

In addition to being offended morally by the excesses of the spoils system, Cleveland understood the change in the requirement of government taking place in the 1880s. The political tradition that "to the victor belongs the spoils" was plainly out of date and had to be abandoned. Still, Cleveland was not unmindful of the need to nourish the political parties, but in his appointments he balanced as honorably as he could the demand for both party loyalty and professional competence. For example, he appointed the assistant in the insurance department to be its director. In filling the ranks of the Railroad Commission, Cleveland chose so carefully that it became a judgment on his stewardship as well as a feather in his political cap that New York State had less organized hostility to the behavior of the railroads than did any other state in the Union.

Cleveland's policies and performance conformed, in general, to the wishes as well as the needs of business—for he recognized that its economic health was essential to the state. At the same time, the governor was attentive to the commitment in the Democratic platform. In his letter of acceptance he had said clearly: "The laboring classes constitute the main part of our population. They should be protected in their efforts to assert their rights when endangered by aggregated capital, and all statutes on the subject should recognize the care of the State for honest toil, and be framed with a view of improving the condition of the workingman."

These words were heeded in the legislature as the long-sought response to the human cost of industrial development got under way. During Cleveland's first year in office, a Bureau of Labor Statistics was created, a remarkable step forward in the assessment of the needs of wage earners. Moreover, the homework system that allowed the making of cigars in tenement houses—often with the help of child labor—was prohibited. And the manufacture of woolen hats by prisoners was ended. Although Cleveland signed and supported heartily these important laws, he was not yet ready for maximum hours regulation. When an effort was afoot to limit the working day of streetcar conductors to twelve hours, Cleveland was firmly opposed.

The "Car Conductors' and Drivers' Bill," it was his argument, would limit the right of workingmen to contract with their employers for any length of day they chose. It would be another generation before such a position was disputed as well as denounced by the U.S. Supreme Court. Cleveland was only moving slowly past the mainstream of public thinking. He was a legalist committed to a legal system not yet able to rein in the cutthroat forces of the marketplace. As his first year drew to a close, he could be satisfied that he had fulfilled the promise he had made on his Inauguration Day to serve the public interest fairly and honestly.

Cleveland worked harder and more earnestly than most elective officials. He was married to his work. Today, he would be labeled a workaholic. Very occasionally he took his fishing rod and tried his luck in a local lake or on an island down the Hudson, often with Dan Manning. They became a familiar sight setting out for a day they expected to end with a string of shad in their bag. Sport clothing had still not been created, and attired in business suits and white dress shirts, their only concession to the outdoors was their broad-brimmed Panama hats. Cleveland did not have many intimate friends, but one of them, S. B. Ward, an Albany doctor, introduced him to the beauty—and the fishing waters—of the Adirondacks.

Generally, however, the governor was at his desk even on Sundays, although on Sunday afternoons he often took on some associates in a few hours of draw poker—with a twenty-five-cent limit. He jested that his father thought it sinful to go fishing on the Lord's day but "he never said anything about draw-poker." On weekdays, Cleveland sometimes worked himself into exhaustion, relieved then by an evening of heavy eating and beer drinking at a nearby tavern, almost invariably in the company of Lamont. It is futile to try to explain the intense devotion to the everlasting pile of papers in his office. To be sure, the virtue of hard work carried over in him from the intense Calvinism of his formative years. Still, although it spoke well of his labors that he was on top of the questions he dealt with, it is also a fact that he did not delegate authority easily.

In a later time, Cleveland might have been regarded dismissively as a colorless man of few words. In his day, though, because he memorized his important speeches, he projected an imposing sense of command. His huge size—five feet eleven inches tall, with a thick short neck, yet weighing about 270 pounds or more—added to his presence. His younger relatives called him, affectionately, Uncle Jumbo. Still, his bulk, in that generation before the advent of weight-control advice, suggested that here was a man of substance, literally and figuratively. And wearing only a mustache—a thick brown one that drooped over his upper lip—at a time when so many major politicians, including the past four presidents, wore beards, he struck many people as a decidedly modern man.

As the kingmakers of the Democratic Party looked ahead to the presidential canvass of 1884, they were sanguine about their chances, and New York was a place to look for a candidate. Chester Arthur was an ailing man. "Accidental" presidents like him did not get nominated on their own: John Tyler, Millard Fillmore, and Andrew Johnson had been unlucky examples. The year 1884 would have no incumbent running for the White House, and the prospects of the party of Jefferson and Jackson never seemed brighter. The time seemed ripe at last to break the hold of the Republicans on the White House. Outwardly, Cleveland seemed oblivious to the main chance about to be his.

At the end of Cleveland's first year in office, even dyed-in-the-wool Republicans had grudgingly to concede that the governor had fulfilled his promise to be honest and true to his commitment that integrity in public office was a worthy requirement of those entrusted with responsibility and authority. The Democratic Party was pleased to think that their man had won salutes in editorial offices throughout the state. Moreover, when the national chieftains of the party began to plan for 1884, as had become their habit, they looked toward the governor's mansion in Albany. Cleveland was too good a political animal to comment on speculation about his future. He concentrated only on the task of governing well. He faced his second year eagerly and less tentatively than in the previous one. The public seemed fully to support his style of governing.

He showed his growing confidence in his address before the Democratic Party convention on the eve of the 1883 elections. Already Democrats had won in Ohio. Cleveland declared in tones that seemed new, for they were crusading tones: "Ohio in the van calls on us to follow. What shall the answer be? The Democracy of New York sends back the ringing assurance that we are on the way, and in a few short days will be at her side, bearing glorious trophies. . . . We shall succeed because we deserve success, because the people are just, and because we bear high aloft the banner of their rights." Whatever Cleveland's thoughts and hopes were, he had work to do in Albany.

In his message to the legislature, he turned his attention to the relation of private corporations to the state and to the public's well-being. Yet again, he was facing one of the new problems of post–Civil War America, one for which there was as yet no satisfactory solution: the policing of the great and profitable corporations chartered by the state: "It is a grave question whether the formation of these artificial bodies ought not to be checked or better regulated, and in some way supervised. At any rate, they should always be kept well in hand and the funds of its citizens should be protected by the State which has invited their investment." This pointed rebuke to the captains of the new industries who treated stockholders' money as their own seems to have made little impression on the public.

But Cleveland continued to tweak the men of wealth. Speaking in New York City at a celebration marking the one hundredth anniversary of the British evacuation of New York, he implored the businesspeople he addressed to take on the cost of maintaining and operating the port of New York. "Are you sure that all the property of this great metropolis, where fortunes, which the farmer vainly works a lifetime to secure, are made and lost in a day, meets with equal fairness, its share of taxation?"

Cleveland's attack on the freewheeling corporations was a nettle that seemed almost daring. He saw minority stockholders as victims of the bloated barons that controlled American big business: "Immense salaries are paid to officers; transactions are consummated by which the directors make money while the rank and file among the stockholders lose it; the honest investor waits for dividends and the directors grow rich. It is suspected, too, that large sums are spent under various disguises in efforts to influence legislation." This bold predication was remarkable for the day, even though the remedy the governor proposed was mild—timid is a better descriptive: an annual report to an appropriate or designated office, where the figures would be studied and audited. If evidence was found of fraud or perjury, the offending corporate officer would be made liable "to refund to the injured stockholders any expenditure which shall be determined improper by the auditing authority." The teeth required to discipline corporations were still not cut, for both the evils of laissez-faire capitalism and the role of the state in regulating it were only beginning to appear in political discussions. Cleveland deserves credit for seeing the dimensions of the problem and venturing to speak of it candidly.

Most of Cleveland's legislative thinking, though, dealt with urban matters—a constant concern of his, with which he was intimately acquainted. Under his leadership, the legislature in 1884 passed a bill depriving New York City's Board of Aldermen of the power to confirm appointments to certain offices and transferred it to the mayor. Cleveland signed the bill although it did not go as far as he wished. Still, the city was put on the road to cleaner government. Even if corrupt deals that had marked the conduct of its affairs continued under constantly changing auspices, his action enhanced his reputation as a fearless officeholder.

Despite the fact that he had not served in the Civil War— it had not been an issue in his various election campaigns— Cleveland understood the veterans' political strength, and he supported bills giving former soldiers and sailors preference in filling jobs on public works projects; he also gratified their wish to preserve the records of their military units.

Endless as paperwork was in his daily schedule, Cleveland took special satisfaction in some of it. He diligently reviewed court records in order to be assured that the tendency of judges to punish criminals excessively was curbed. He regarded his power to issue pardons as one of the most important, one that tested both his judgment as a lawyer and his instinct as a religious man to whom mercy was a value.

It should not go unnoticed that preserving the public lands had his attention. Under the general rubric of "conservation" the movement was already under way on the national level— Yellowstone National Park had been established in 1873, and the pioneering theorist of conservation, George Perkins Marsh, had already made converts to the cause. The legislature, with Cleveland's hearty approval, set aside lands in the vicinity of Niagara Falls deemed necessary to preserving the scenery. Already economic pressure in the area of the falls had been growing, and private interests had acquired the little islands nearby. They were being used to set up factories, and in order to make them accessible, roads had been built that scarred the landscape and damaged the forests. The restoration work at the falls was quickly known, and the area became a tourist magnet, especially for honeymooners. The spectacular beauty of the site was enhanced by a comparable Canadian renewal plan on the opposite side of the river.

Cleveland was in the vanguard of the advocates for the preservation and protection of the Adirondacks, which was now a preferred place for the rare days of relaxation that he took. His notable efforts were a foretaste of those that soon fascinated the country under the leadership of Theodore Roosevelt. As a member of the state assembly, Roosevelt had approved Cleveland's initiative. In his turn, Cleveland had his eye on the young Roosevelt, who sponsored the bill creating the state civil service system. When it had passed, Cleveland appointed a list of notable citizens to be members of the new civil service commission.

Clearly, Cleveland, for all his instinctive conservatism, was attuned to the new needs of the state and the country. In keeping with the tendency of the day, he not only helped to create a better civil service system for New York, but he never slackened in supporting improvements in education. When he visited a school, he could charm his hearers as he did when he spoke at Albany High School. He assured the students that he would not trouble them with a big speech—likely recalling his own boredom on occasions when politicians interrupted his day in school.

As Cleveland's term drew to a close, he had compiled an enviable record on which his successor, David Bennett Hill, who had been the lieutenant governor, might build. To the last of his days in office, Cleveland kept attending to his duties, working past midnight and often eating alone at his desk what passed for an evening meal. As the year 1885 opened and the new state administration prepared to take over the executive mansion, Cleveland moved to a private apartment in Albany. Only three years out of the mayoralty of Buffalo, he turned his thoughts toward a new challenge—the presidency of the United States.

4

The Making of a President

The presidential election of 1884, like that of 1880, took place without an incumbent running for reelection. When Chester Arthur became president following the assassination of President Garfield, the political reformers were tremulous. But Chet Arthur had had a very respectable administration—to the complete surprise of many people who regarded him as an unreconstructible spoilsman.

Arthur had been a pro-Grant delegate and lieutenant to Roscoe Conkling at the Republican convention held in 1880 in Chicago. As a Stalwart Republican, Arthur became available when Garfield, the nominee for president, decided that Conkling's disappointed followers deserved to be placated by putting one of their number on the ticket. Representative Levi P. Morton of New York, a dominant banker and real estate investor, was offered the second place but turned it down. Arthur gleefully accepted it, telling the angry Conkling—who had pleaded with him also to reject the invitation—that the thought of being vice president went beyond even the wildest dreams of his youth.

Now, however, after completing Garfield's term he was in bad odor with fellow Republicans. Stalwarts regarded him as a turncoat, even though he had broken with Garfield and sided with Conkling in the fight over the control of the patronage.

Arthur tried hard to get the nomination for president in his own right, but winning it without the support of the Stalwarts was out of the question—and they would not give it to him. Moreover, other Republicans did not trust him, because he had never kissed and made up with them. On top of this, his advocacy of tariff reform, now emerging as an important national issue, had alienated some of the big business backers of the party. Further, he was not a popular figure with the public at large, which regarded him as indolent and careless in the conduct of his office. Nor did he satisfy the new breed of newspaper reporters who catered to the demand for the details of politicians' private lives. He had bluntly snorted, "I may be President of the United States, but my private life is nobody's damned business." Known to some as the Dude President and as Elegant Arthur, he was said to own twenty-five overcoats—a man more interested in himself than in the people at large. Cleveland watched the decline of the New York Republicans and bided his time.

The Republican convention met on June 6, 1884, once more in Chicago. The showplace site on the shore of Lake Michigan was the magnificent Inter-State Exposition Building, an immense iron-and-glass structure opened in 1873. Designed by W. W. Boyington, its erection celebrated the recovery of the city from the Great Fire of '71.

The nomination of James Gillespie Blaine of Maine was a foregone conclusion. The brilliant son of a county clerk in West Brownsville, Pennsylvania, he was born in 1830. He graduated with high honors from Washington and Jefferson College in 1847. Upon his marriage he moved to his wife's hometown of Augusta, Maine. Having become the editor of the *Kennebec Journal*, his influence enabled him to found the state's Republican Party, of which he became the leader. After service in the state legislature, the people sent him to Washington, where he served in the House of Representatives for thirteen years and from 1869 to 1875 was the Speaker. A supporter of the Radical Republicans, he voted for the impeachment of President Johnson. Dubbed the Plumed Knight, he was a candidate for his party's presidential nomination in 1876. But his candidacy was annihilated by the bombshell of the so-called Mulligan letters. They showed that while Speaker, he did a valuable favor for the Little Rock and Fort Smith Railroad and was rewarded with a secret arrangement to sell the bonds of the line at a handsome commission.

Soon after the disclosure, Blaine suffered a physical collapse that seemed to end his career. Nevertheless, he had been elected to the Senate, and he remained a perennial hopeful for the White House. In 1880 his partisans were active on his behalf once again. Known now as one of the Half-Breeds, that is, the moderately conservative wing of his party, he was blocked off when it turned to Garfield.

In Garfield's brief time in the White House, Blaine was the secretary of state. By 1884, Conkling being in eclipse, no one stood in Blaine's way as he claimed what he regarded as his birthright, the party's highest honor. The only living impediment to his place at the top of the ticket was General William Tecumseh Sherman. Sherman turned down the opportunity with the deathless declaration: "If nominated, I will not accept. If elected, I will not serve."

Blaine was confident that he could count on the votes of Roman Catholics traditionally wedded to the Democratic Party: his mother had been an Irish Catholic, and his sister was the Mother Superior of a convent school. On the first ballot, out of a possible 818 votes, Blaine led over the runner-up, President Arthur, by 334½ to 278, just 78 short of the nomination. In third place was George Franklin Edmunds of Vermont, who stood for reform and the rehabilitation of the party. Alas, the party was not yet ready for revitalization. On the fourth ballot, Blaine, having advanced steadily on the subsequent roll calls, went over the top with 541 votes as Arthur fell to 207 and the favorite sons were sacrificed to the selection of Blaine. Blaine's stained public record, his continued adherence to bloody-shirt politics, and his identification as a spoilsman were burdens he carried into the campaign.

Meanwhile, Cleveland offered steadily impressive evidence of his devotion to the advancement of New York State—"the leader of all the States," as he called it. There was a forceful directness in his paean to New York in the speech he delivered on the Fourth of July, 1884, to mark the completion of Buffalo's Civil War monument.

No examples of civic devotion were more important, north and south, than its war monuments in every town square. They were a token of the desire that never more must the nation be riven and indulge in such a bloodbath—nor its heroes be forgotten. As Cleveland said: "There came a time when discord reached the family circle of States threatening the nation's life. Can we forget how wildly New York sprang forward to protect and preserve what she had done so much to create and build up? Four hundred and fifty thousand men left her borders to stay the tide of destruction." The governor's words gave evidence of a passion stirring beneath his unbending exterior. His emphasis on the "nation's life"—as well as that of the state—was a token of his widening outlook. It contributed to the growing sentiment that Cleveland was ready, that the hour and the man were about to meet.

Few Americans had seen a picture of him; indeed, most Americans did not know what the president or the nominees looked like. The halftone method of reproducing pictures on the pages of newspapers had not yet been invented. Yet Cleveland's reputation for integrity was spreading from one end of the land to the other. His partisans later would say that he was the candidate of the people before he became the candidate of his party. What was most remarkable was that unlike his immediate predecessors, Hayes, Garfield, and Arthur, he was not the choice of the party bosses. Nor was he a war hero, like Grant and Lincoln, or even on a lower level of heroism, like Hayes and Garfield.

Cleveland was the symbol of high-mindedness and devoted care in local governance. Wherever people were weary of hoping to have government for the people but finding instead government for the politicians, they thought immediately of the broad-shouldered governor of New York as their champion. Even in states with favorite sons, Cleveland had his backers. It seemed a vindication of democracy that without fanfare or a concerted campaign to put him across, Cleveland's virtues singled him out.

The Democrats gathered in Chicago on July 8 in the Exposition Building, where the Republicans had held their convention two weeks earlier. Its main hall had since then been refitted and redecorated. The pillars and the gallery were festooned in fresh bunting and overhead floated garlands of red, white, and blue banners. The delegates drifted in singly and in small groups, and by noon the gallery was still barely half filled. But at twelve-forty, only a bit late, William Henry Barnum of Connecticut, chairman of the Democratic National Committee, called the convention to order. Just below the raised platform were arranged the tables assigned to the representatives of the press. And below them in twenty rows were the seats of the delegates— 820 in all—with each state's place plainly marked. The states were arranged alphabetically. The Alabamans were on the left side of the hall, the delegates from Maine on the right. In the middle sat the New Yorkers, 72 strong. To the left and right of the delegates clustered the army of partisans eager to cheer for their favorites.

Most of the big names of the party were on hand. From the Senate were Wade Hampton of South Carolina, a Confederate general and former governor of South Carolina; Lucius Quintus Cincinnatus Lamar of Mississippi, another proud former Confederate who would end his long career on the U.S. Supreme Court; George H. Pendleton of Ohio, the author of the act bearing his name that laid the basis for the federal civil service system; and Allen G. Thurman, also of Ohio, who would later be an unsuccessful candidate for the vice presidency.

From the House of Representatives came William Mutchler of Pennsylvania, a veteran of Democratic presidential conventions, and Abram S. Hewitt of New York, who shortly would become mayor of New York City. As these worthies entered the hall and were recognized by their friends, they were cheered to the echo, louder and louder, said one observer, "first like the patter of a summer shower and then rising to the roar of a hurricane." Thurman was a special favorite. When he made his appearance, an exuberant Californian bellowed: "The California delegation, after traveling twenty-five hundred miles, catches its first glimpse of Paradise in the person of Allen G. Thurman." Confederate yells broke out throughout the amphitheater when Hampton entered it and looked for his seat.

The proceedings began with an invocation offered by the Reverend D. C. Marquis of the Northwestern Theological Seminary. It was a call for peaceful deliberations, a sentiment quickly echoed by Barnum, who then presented Governor Richard B. Hubbard of Texas as the temporary chairman of the convention. Hubbard, known as an excellent parliamentarian, spoke with the deep accent of his native Georgia, although he had spent most of his adult life in Texas. He rang the changes on the election of 1876, unabashedly labeling it an election stolen by perjury and fraud. Although he invited attention to the honorable way in which Samuel Tilden and Thomas Hendricks had accepted the verdict of the Electoral Commission that made Rutherford Hayes the president, the delegates hardly heard this mention. They were on their feet stamping and rending the air at the top of their lungs.

Now, he said, the party was ready to reclaim the White House. Its candidate's very name would be its platform. There would be an end to robbery in high places, and, he insisted, the surplus in the Treasury would not be allowed to accumulate. Hubbard had the delegates standing and screaming themselves hoarse as he urged united support for the nominee. He ended on the high note that anyone who failed in that duty to the party would not be a good Democrat and surely not a patriot.

Following this stirring call to the faithful, the convention proceeded to its work. First, though, Tom Grady of New York's contingent, still smarting over having been denied at Cleveland's hands the leadership of the state senate, was now seeking revenge. He introduced a motion to abolish the long-standing unit rule by which New York State's delegation was obliged to cast its entire vote for the candidate approved by a majority of its members. After considerable speech making that masqueraded as discussion, the motion was rejected by a vote of 463 to 322. Those voting in favor of the proposal had more than New York on their minds: they were part of the "stop Cleveland" forces, and they would soon present several alternative names. The victory for Cleveland on this vote, though, was a promising portent; he was the clear front-runner, firmly backed by the reformers and the sound-money men.

The second day of the convention would tell the tale, for names were to be put in nomination. Following the invocation, Colonel William F. Vilas of Wisconsin was named as chairman. Vilas, a hero of the 36th Wisconsin Regiment, earned national notice with his eloquent speech at the reunion of the Army of the Tennessee in Chicago in 1879, which President Grant had attended. It is said that his address was so successful that Robert Ingersoll, one of the most powerful orators of the day, scheduled to speak next, was more than a little irritated at having to follow Vilas at the podium.

Vilas's speech did not disappoint. He touched all the bases, including an uninhibited attack upon the Republicans whom he accused of still waving the bloody shirt. "To a country which rejoices in restored unity and concord they tender the renewal of sectional strife," he charged. He insisted that the Republicans, instead of recognizing that the people were "demanding deliverance from dishonor and corruption," were offering only "the gilded arts of skillful demagogy." On and on he went with a catalogue of Republican sins that only the most committed Democrats could accept. Yet he was stirring the blood of the true believers. After some resolutions relating to the party's platform were offered and passed along to the platform committee, nominations for president began.

The first few states in the alphabet passed. Then Delaware offered the name of Senator Thomas F. Bayard. The spokesman for Indiana, Thomas Hendricks, brought the delegates to their feet hurraying and waving their banners and hats. He was one of the beloved figures in the convention, not yet certain that he would shortly be its choice to be vice president. Since he could not put himself forward as a favorite son, he placed in nomination Joseph E. McDonald, who had served as senator, and like Bayard had been defeated in a run for governor.

Other familiar names would be placed in nomination before the roll call was completed: John G. Carlisle of Kentucky, Speaker of the House of Representatives; George Hoadley, governor of Ohio; and Samuel J. Randall of Pennsylvania, a former Speaker. As each was named in turn and heralded not only as a sure winner but imagined also as a perfect president, rabid friends cheered with abandon, according to custom.

When the state of New York was called, thunderous cheers of great expectation filled the hall, for Cleveland's name was about to be put in the running. Delegates excitedly jumped up and down waving handkerchiefs and canes. Many hurled hats and coats into the air—neither being needed in Chicago's intense summer heat. The designated spokesman was Daniel N. Lockwood, the member of the House who represented Buffalo. He had been the district attorney of Erie County, and it was he who only four years before had nominated Cleveland to be mayor of his city. As he rose to speak, a hush fell upon the assemblage. Alas, he was an unimaginative young man, and he made an unimaginative speech, fortunately fairly brief.

The words were right but uninspiring. He recalled first his long friendship with Cleveland, and then he pointed to Cleveland's unblemished performance as mayor and then as governor of New York. The people who sent Cleveland to Albany, he shouted, "knew that that meant honest government; it meant pure government; it meant Democratic government." In his peroration he summed up: "Cleveland's candidacy before this Convention is offered upon the ground of his honor, his integrity, his wisdom, and his Democracy." The wild ovation that punctuated the speech was for its sentiment, not for the impression the words had made. They were sincere and truthful but not quotable. But they proved sufficient.

As the seconding speeches began, the Cleveland supporters knew they must scotch the canard being floated by the Tammany contingent that Cleveland could not win Irish-American votes. Carter Harrison, the mayor of Chicago, in his stern seconding speech, vigorously denounced the assertion, and added that it was a slander also to say that the Catholic church would work against Cleveland. He could not resist adding that Blaine was the one who must look to his interests because, Harrison said, so many Irish-Americans resented the deaf ear he turned to them when he was secretary of state and they were pleading for McSweeney, the Irish rebel languishing in an English jail. Then Tom Grady got the floor, his cohorts, led by "Honest" John Kelly, having shouted incessantly in unison, "Grady! Grady! Grady!" At last, the chair had yielded.

Grady's words were syrupy and full of reasonableness as he contended that he would be delighted to second Cleveland's nomination but "I know, and I believe I can show you, that he cannot carry the State of New York." As he continued his imprecation, shouts of "Put him out!" came from the galleries. At this point the chair ruled Grady out of order. Grady could see that an appeal against the ruling would be futile. Tactfully, Dan Manning rose to ask the chair to allow Grady to proceed. This act of magnanimity was not lost on the fascinated assemblage. Thereupon Grady continued with his diatribe and proceeded to second the nomination of Joseph McDonald, the Indiana man. Bourke Cockran, a Grady ally, now took up the widespread belief that the mantle of the beloved Samuel J. Tilden was about to fall on Cleveland: "When the mantle of a giant falls upon a dwarf," intoned Cockran, "he is bound to be smothered." The attack was wounding.

When the convention reconvened the next day, the fire Grady had set was still smoldering. With lively anticipation by the delegates, Edward Stuyvesant Bragg, a native New Yorker transplanted to Wisconsin, stood up to second Cleveland's nomination. Bragg's

middle name bespoke his heritage. He had been a Union cavalry-
man, rising to the rank of brigadier general, and subsequently
served in Congress. Now out of office, he was remembered
for the fiery speeches he delivered on the floor of the House,
and for the independence he showed in often voting with the
Republicans. No one in Congress had a sharper tongue than he.
The convention was all ears as he began.

He swiftly roused the audience, arguing that young men for
whom he said he was speaking were eager for new leadership.
The time had come to retire the old warhorses. Cleveland was
no "holiday reformer," he was the real McCoy. Bragg went on to
say that people love Cleveland "and they respect him not only
for himself, for his character, for his integrity and judgment and
iron will, but they love him most of all for the enemies he has
made." John Kelly, the leader of the Tammany cohort, rushed to
the platform and declared that he was pleased by the compliment. Grady, seated just below the rostrum, was seen to grow
beet-red with rage and shouted, "On behalf of his enemies, I
accept the sentiment." Bragg continued, responding to the
shouted call of one delegate: "Give 'em a little more grape." The
convention hall erupted into bedlam, the vast body of delegates
not only screaming its support for Cleveland but also relishing
the assault on Irish Tammany—a way of flaying New York City,
already envied and feared in the hinterland for its unconstrained
cosmopolitanism. Bragg, the old soldier, offered parting words:
"Our ides of November will not be a Waterloo, but the glorious
sun of Austerlitz."

It was agreed that the balloting would not begin until the
platform was adopted, a process that ground on as day turned
into night. Then, at long last, the balloting got under way. When
the tally was announced at one-thirty in the morning, Cleveland
led with 392 votes, followed by Bayard with 170, Thurman with
88, and a scattering for the other names. Exhausted by their
yelling and demonstrating, some of the delegates left the hall.
Manning and the other Cleveland managers were afraid that
because some of those departing were Cleveland supporters, a

second ballot would reveal a retreat from their candidate. So they engineered a recess of the convention until the following morning.

Grady and his claque believed they could still defeat Cleveland by selecting a dark horse. They agreed upon Hendricks. In the conspiracy were the diabolical Benjamin Butler, still fantasizing that one day he might sit in the White House, "Honest" John Kelly, and Hendricks himself. But a Cleveland spy was in the discussions of the plot that lasted through the night, and in the morning Manning knew what was up. Before many of the delegates were out of bed, they were roused by the Cleveland men to get them on the convention floor. Meanwhile, the plotters were hoping to stampede the convention for Hendricks. Their enthusiasm frightened the Cleveland forces, especially when Indiana shifted from McDonald to Hendricks. But Pennsylvania saved the day when its spokesman withdrew the name of Samuel Randall and threw its entire vote to Cleveland. The insurrection was over, and Cleveland piled up the necessary two-thirds of the ballots. The final tally was as Manning had dreamed and planned:

Whole number of votes	820
Required for a choice	547
Grover Cleveland	683
Thomas Bayard	81½
Thomas Hendricks	45½
Samuel Randall	4
Allen Thurman	4
Joseph McDonald	2

The convention concluded with the perfunctory business of naming a vice presidential candidate. After brief displays of enthusiasm for a handful of favorite sons, Hendricks was the choice of the party managers, and his nomination went through by acclamation. The band struck up the music for "He's a Jolly Good Fellow," while all eyes were on the oil painting of Cleveland that stood at the rostrum, adorned below by a huge horseshoe-shaped floral piece. Then the entire convention responded to the band's rendition of Bourgeois's "Praise God, From Whom All Blessings Flow" and, saintlike, sang its verses in high spirits. The delegates behind their state banners marched up and down the aisles and finally massed their standards in front of the platform. The names Cleveland and Hendricks were on everybody's lips, and, confident of victory, the cheers went on and on, subsiding only slowly.

The campaign was in full swing almost immediately. The party platforms seemed indistinguishable. Neither side was seeking dispute on public policy. The Republicans were calling for a high tariff, not for revenue, but to protect the livelihood of working people; curbs on the immigration of Chinese men and women; the enforcement of the eight-hour day; and regulation of the railroads. The Democrats were supporting a tariff that would protect infant industries, the right of laboring people to organize, and, in foreign affairs, the new concept of Pan-Americanism. They, too, advocated restricting Chinese immigration.

Beyond the anti-Chinese sentiment, racism was rampant in the country. Cleveland, himself, never shook off the prejudices of his era toward black people. The recently freed slaves everywhere met discrimination and segregation and, increasingly in the South, lynching. On the frontier, military force was being deployed against Indians almost to the point of genocide. Immigrants from Ireland and southern and eastern Europe were greeted with open hostility, except when their brawn was needed for society's backbreaking work. Such blatant national misconduct pricked neither the conscience nor the concern of the major parties. And public opinion too was loudly silent about it. The campaign, therefore, one of the most furiously fought in history, avoided these pressing and shameful matters. It revolved, rather, around the moral qualifications of the standard-bearers.

The Democrats knew they had chosen a man who would not rock the boat. It had not been lost on the delegates that

Cleveland had strong appeal to the Mugwump Republicans who would not go for Blaine. The Mugwumps—from the Algonquian word meaning "Big Chief"—wanted reforms, but not radical ones. (Their critics scornfully said they were impotent straddlers, their "mug" on one side of the fence and their "wump" on the other.) Politicians were ultimately pleased to know that when Cleveland spoke of civil service reform he did not mean that all political appointees would be at risk.

The party honchos had confidence in Cleveland's conservatism. Furthermore, with a gruff courtliness that some people found charming but others saw as a sign of detachment, he was an ideal man to have his campaign restrained and managed by hands other than his own. In him, then, the party believed it had a compatible and even suggestible candidate. The men who stood behind him have often been dubbed Bourbon Democrats.

Bourbon Democracy was a name inspired not by the Kentucky whiskey but by the backward-looking restored monarchy in France, of which Talleyrand, the irrepressible French diplomat, had quipped that its people had learned nothing and forgotten nothing. It was a form of Jeffersonianism dedicated to small, mostly inert government, aimed more at protecting business than promoting the substantial needs of the larger population. For sixteen years in the post–Civil War era, the party had failed every four years to win the White House. Had it been able to make itself the voice of the embattled rural folk and the urban proletariat, it might have wooed them away from the Republican Party. Instead, the party chieftains allied themselves with the rising factory owners of the so-called New South and, benefiting from the iron grip that these businessmen had on their section's electorate, felt no impulse to befriend mill hands or freedmen working in the cotton fields.

Cleveland's nomination came in the era before candidates addressed the convention that named them. Lincoln, for instance, had been playing ball with his children in Springfield in 1860, when news of his nomination in Chicago was brought to him.

Cleveland was in his office in Albany where he heard a cannon volley heralding the news from the convention hall. "They are firing a salute in your honor, Governor," one of his staff called out. "Do you think so?" Cleveland is said to have responded, as he continued to work at his desk. A few minutes later when a telephone call—still a modern miracle—confirmed the news, the governor's response was typical of him, "By Jove, that is something, isn't it?" Words and manner were restrained with a vengeance.

That evening a crowd gathered in downtown Albany and marched on the mansion to serenade him. Cleveland emerged to deliver the first of the handful of speeches he gave in the entire campaign. His words were unadorned: "I am, of course, aware that you pay no compliment to a citizen, and present no personal tribute, but that you have come to demonstrate your loyalty and devotion to a cause in which you heartily believe." Then he went after the Republicans—mildly. He knew he must win the hearts—and votes—of moderates: "Parties may be so long in power, and may become so arrogant and careless of the interest of the people, as to grow heedless of their responsibility to their masters." This serious mistake must be rectified, he declared. And he concluded: "Let us, then, enter upon the campaign, now fairly opened . . . with a solid front, to do battle for better government, confidently, courageously, always honorably, and with a firm reliance upon the intelligence and patriotism of the American people." From this sample, it was clear there would be no rabble-rousing, no call for a battle to the death.

On August 18, Cleveland received formal notification of his nomination. His response, it seems to us today, was ponderous and vapid—even though he had retired to the Adirondacks especially to prepare it. No innovator would he be, he said. His view of the presidency was simple: "It should be remembered that the office of the President is essentially executive in its nature. The laws enacted by the legislative branch of the government, the Chief Executive is bound faithfully to enforce." When a party states its principles in its platform, he went on, the candidate need not say more. He spoke feelingly of what it means that America enjoys a "government of the people." He pointed to the ability of citizens to go to the polls and "avenge truth betrayed and pledges broken." To that end, nothing would be more efficacious "than an amendment disqualifying the President from re-election." He closed by greeting his audience as "co-workers in a noble cause." In the way of recent Democratic candidates, his appeal for civil service reform was clear and unqualified. He made no mention of the tariff that was also agitating political waters. In sum, the undistinguished speech elevated no spirits.

His antagonist, Blaine, an accomplished speaker, lauded the existing high tariff as a protection for working people. In keeping with his longtime commitment to courting Latin American trade, he spoke for it once more. Recognizing, as thoughtful fellow Republicans did, that the time for waving the bloody shirt was past, he held his tongue. He went beyond Cleveland in expressing devotion to civil service reform, proposing that the new dispensation apply to consular appointments, and that four-year appointments that ended with a president's term be abandoned so that the job roster was not wiped clean at the end of each administration.

The campaign began according to pattern. The nominees were expected to behave with detachment and even to feign indifference to the outcome. Self-promotion was off the table, a difficult condition for Blaine, whose public massaging of his ego was a hallmark of his career. But his commanding presence and his elegant attire made him an idol among the party faithful. Stylish clothing in that generation was only for the few: it conveyed to the world a sense of the importance and self-confidence of the wearer. A magnetic personality, Blaine was at his best before a large audience rather than a small one. Some of his hearers regarded him as superior on the stump to any of his contemporaries. He often complained of being indisposed after a particularly powerful address, perhaps because his performances were exhausting. Adding to his appeal was that he was known as a faithful family man, he and his wife raising a brood of seven children.

After his nomination, Blaine had retreated to his home in Maine, where he was said to be working on the second volume of his memoirs, *Twenty Years of Congress from Lincoln to Garfield*, the first of which was just reaching the bookstores. Like Cleveland, he was acting as expected, seeming to leave to fate alone the outcome of the campaign. In reality, he was spending much of his time micromanaging it, greeting visiting delegations and showing his knowledge of men and politics superior to that of even his most experienced helpers. For his part, Cleveland was quietly hopeful—even confident—and attentive to guidance from Manning and Lamont as had become his wont. Well aware of his colorlessness as a public speaker, he was relying on his usual pose of modesty and his history of allowing honor and respect to come to him unbidden.

Accustomed to attending state fairs and rallies of Civil War veterans, Cleveland did not have to adjust much to his new role. And since being on the campaign trail was still not an American custom, his appearances did not always call for speech making. Nor was the pressing of the flesh, de rigueur in twentieth-century campaigns, required as a means of vote getting. On October 2 the city of Buffalo, adorned with banners and lanterns, formally greeted its famous son. Then Cleveland made his way to New York City, where a parade along Fifth Avenue allowed the Democrats to show off their candidate—notably without the hoopla that Tammany would usually provide.

Behind the public appearances, party operatives were raising money for strategic vote buying. Because the Pendleton Act and similar legislation in the states had ended the ability of political bosses to dun jobholders for contributions, money raisers turned to the leaders of industry. On the Republican side, the man who passed the hat was an old Blaine supporter, the Pittsburgh steel magnate Benjamin F. Jones of Jones & Laughlin, a firm that enjoyed the benefits of high tariffs. The Democrats had selected

William Barnum as a money raiser. His successful investments were legion, and, it was said, he knew everybody of wealth. Jones and Barnum provided the window dressing for subordinates who actually rattled the tin cup in front of likely donors. Of course, the candidates were presumed to know nothing of the appeals for money made for their sake. In order to reach out to so-called independents, one Democratic newspaper established a popular subscription in which as little as one dollar was welcome. The device enabled the party to suggest it hugged to its bosom the ordinary people of the country.

Cleveland, meanwhile, was showing himself in but a few places not far from home. On October 28 he spoke in Newark, New Jersey. His radiation of warmth was scant: he had come, he said, in response to the wishes of many friends, and "a number of those who, as neighbors, remember my family, if not me." He continued: "I do not wish to attempt any false pretense by claiming that ever since the day when, a very small boy, I left the State, I have languished in an enforced absence and longed to tread again its soil; and yet I may say, without affectation, that though the way of life has led me far from the place of my birth, the names of Caldwell and Newark, and the memories connected with those places are as fresh as ever." Such roundabout phrasing was not in the common political style of the day but in the journalistic style, meant to be read rather than spoken. With such solemnity he papered over the pressing questions of tariff, currency, and monopoly. It made not a whit of difference: he was cheered enthusiastically.

His henchmen, finding no significant issue to duel over with the Republicans, commenced a campaign of personal attacks. They exhumed the old story of Blaine's financial relationship to the Little Rock and Fort Smith Railroad and his efforts to deny it that had long delayed his acceptability as the party's candidate for president. The incriminating words "Burn this letter," in one of the now unearthed Mulligan missives, began to turn up in Democratic newspapers. The Republicans were both

dismayed and discouraged, for Cleveland, their sturdy opponent, was the very symbol of rectitude and incorruptibility. But
happily they found a chink in his puritan armor.

It was revealed to them on July 21, only two weeks after the
Democratic convention, when newsboys began hawking the
Buffalo Evening Telegraph with its incredible front-page article
headed:

A TERRIBLE TALE
A Dark Chapter in a Public Man's History
The Pitiful Story of Maria Halpin and Governor Cleveland's Son

The straitlaced Cleveland notably unconfident with women
of his own class undoubtedly enjoyed bantering with the wait-
resses in the taverns he patronized. That he weighed at least 250
pounds was the only outward evidence that he ever enjoyed
himself—that he was a trencherman and beer swiller. But this
story implied the coexistence of a licentious reprobate who
unfeelingly deceived the public. The details, on their face, were
shocking. The article spoke of how Cleveland had seduced
Halpin and, when she became pregnant, led her to believe he
was going to marry her. Instead, he forced her to commit the
baby to an orphan asylum, and the fallen woman was obliged to
leave town. Her seducer, the paper went on, remained publicly a
paragon of virtue and goodness. These "facts" seemed to give the
lie to Cleveland's pontifical assertion of long before: "It is no
credit to me to do right. I am under no temptation to do wrong."

The facts are somewhat different. Maria Halpin was a comely
young widow from Pennsylvania who, leaving two children
behind, had come to Buffalo from Jersey City in 1871 at the age
of thirty-three—a year younger than Cleveland. Tall, attractive,
and winsome, able to speak French, she had found employment
in a dry-goods store and quickly attained a responsible position.
A parishioner of the fashionable St. John's Episcopal Church,
she almost immediately had prominent friends. Possibly Cleveland was seduced as well as the seducer. When the child was

born, Halpin began to drink heavily and to neglect the infant. Alarmed, Cleveland had his friend, Roswell L. Burrows, a county judge, look into the matter. He arranged for Halpin to be committed to the Providence Asylum—an institution for mentally deranged people run by the Sisters of Charity. The little boy was sent to the Protestant Orphan Asylum, where Cleveland promised to pay through Burrows the monthly cost of five dollars. Cleveland also persuaded Halpin to leave town, setting her up in business in Niagara Falls.

Pining for her child and still disappointed that she had not been able to snare Cleveland in marriage, she returned to Buffalo in 1876 and, after failing to recover him legally, kidnapped the youngster from the orphanage. Burrows once again played the Good Samaritan: he returned the boy to the asylum from which he was later adopted by a respectable family in town. Halpin disappeared, although years later, during Cleveland's second term as president, she wrote to him for money.

That Cleveland had been involved with Halpin was known in official circles in Buffalo, because he had had the help of detectives and others in arranging for Halpin to be committed, and for the boy to be adopted. Moreover, Cleveland had mentioned his "woman scrape" to a New York Democratic leader at the time of the convention in Chicago, and even though Tammany people knew of it, they made nothing of the story. The name of Cleveland's friend Oscar Folsom was central to the tale. Halpin had named her infant Oscar Folsom Cleveland.

Although Cleveland never acknowledged the child to be his, as we see, he had contributed to the boy's support. Possibly Miss Halpin did not know who the father was and had selected Cleveland because he was the most likely or because he was the only bachelor among the possibilities. Folsom was a man about town who sought his pleasures of the night. In all likelihood, Cleveland accepted responsibility because of his affection for Folsom, who was killed in a traffic accident in 1875. The gesture honored the memory of his friend and spared his widow and daughter from shame.

Because the *Telegraph* had a reputation as a scandal sheet,
many people dismissed its lurid report. But the creditable *Boston
Journal* was another matter. It sent to Buffalo a reporter who discovered confirmation of the damning account and published it.
The principal source was the Reverend George H. Ball of the
Hudson Street Free Baptist Church. Ball asserted that respectable people never allowed Cleveland into their homes, that
he was a noted whoremonger, regularly frequenting Buffalo's
fleshpots, and that his roistering and carousing were legendary.
"Women now married and anxious to cover the sins of their
youth have been his victims, and are now alarmed lest their relations with him shall be exposed. . . . Abundant rumors impli-
cate him at Albany, and well-authenticated facts convict him
at Buffalo." Ball insisted that the awful fate of Maria Halpin
was not a solitary incident and that Cleveland even after becoming governor had not "abated his lecheries." Word spread that
one night Cleveland was so drunk with his law partner Oscar
Folsom that they lost control of the horses drawing their carriage and that that was how Folsom was thrown from it and
killed.

When Cleveland's longtime chum Charles Goodyear asked
him what the Democrats' public response should be, Cleveland
answered in a telegram that was simple and direct: "Tell the
truth," three words that remain to this day the gold standard
reply, not always adopted, for a politician discovered in an
embarrassing predicament. Cleveland was infuriated when an
embellishment of the story, ascribed to another old friend,
Charles McCune, editor of the *Buffalo Courier,* explained that
Cleveland's acceptance of responsibility for the Halpin boy had
been to shield the name of his deceased friend Folsom. Cleveland, in high dudgeon, wrote to another friend: "Now is this man
crazy or does he wish to ruin somebody? Is he fool enough to
suppose for a moment that if such was the truth (which it is
not, so far as the motive for silence is concerned) that I would
permit my dead friend's memory to suffer for my sake? And
Mrs. Folsom and her daughter at my house at this very time!"

Despite the disclaimer, this explanation was at the heart of the very popular mawkish novel *The Honorable Peter Stirling, and What People Thought of Him* by Paul Leicester Ford, which was published in 1894. Ford vehemently denied his book was a roman à clef, but the public read it as such, and it went through countless editions in the half century after its appearance. In truth, Cleveland had a double reason for shielding Folsom's name, for he was smitten with love for Folsom's daughter, Frances, just turned twenty years old. Although she did not yet know of Cleveland's intense feelings, she must have guessed the significance of the bouquet of flowers he sent her from the executive mansion every week. He had gazed on her lovingly from the day of her birth. Indeed, he had bought her her first baby carriage. No novelist could have concocted such a scenario.

Cleveland, who had been feted and cheered by his fellow Buffalonians after his nomination, was nonplussed by his treatment at the hands of erstwhile neighbors. Never again did he feel comfortable in the city, and during the rest of his life he visited it only three times—always for ceremonial events he could not avoid. As the excitement of the "revelation" finally died down and even the Reverend Ball apologized for his outbursts, Cleveland sheltered in the Albany mansion in humiliation. He made only a handful of appearances during the campaign, unlike Blaine, who traveled up and down the eastern part of the country drumming up fresh backing like a man possessed, and delivering more than four hundred speeches in a six-week period.

Still, Cleveland's forthright public reaction to the scandal symbolized his honesty and integrity. And many voters seem to have accepted the suggestion of a Democratic leader who advised that "we should elect Mr. Cleveland to the public office he is so admirably qualified to fill, and remand Mr. Blaine to the private life he is so eminently fitted to adorn." We can never know how many voters—all men in that era—felt sympathy for Cleveland because they had been in comparable circumstances themselves. That Cleveland had not served in the war was not raised as an issue because Blaine had not been in uniform either.

Democrats dug up the information that the Blaines had married secretly because Mrs. Blaine was pregnant, and only later married publicly. Cleveland would have no part of this smear or of others that he was informed of by mail. "The other side can have the monopoly of all the dirt in this campaign," he said. Given his few public appearances, it was left to the state organizations to fire up the party faithful with torchlight processions and military-type parades. Both parties filled their war chests through persistent calls on business leaders. The Democrats, being better organized, raised more money to pay for these popular outpourings than did the Republicans.

The Republican crowds that often paraded behind baby carriages sometimes chanted:

> *Ma! Ma! Where's my pa?*
> *Gone to the White House, ha, ha, ha.*

The Democratic faithful, no less vocal, marched to:

> *Blaine, Blaine, Blaine,*
> *The continental liar from the state of Maine.*
> *Burn this letter!*

Newspapers were learning to treat politics as a form of public entertainment. But to discriminating citizens, the clatter offered proof that the great republic that had only a few years earlier celebrated the centennial of its birth was betraying its lofty promise.

It was generally understood that the candidate who captured New York would be the victor. To win this prize, Blaine, though exhausted by his exertions and eager to relax in Maine, decided to canvass New York from end to end. He even sought the help of his old adversary Roscoe Conkling, who responded contemptuously: "I do not engage in criminal practice." After crisscrossing the state, Blaine arrived in New York City on October 29. He addressed a group of Protestant clergymen in a hastily assembled meeting at the Fifth Avenue Hotel. The leading ministers were not there, because the invitation flyer, in bad taste, referred to the Ball canard of two months earlier. The chairman was the Reverend Samuel D. Burchard, veteran pastor of the Murray Hill Presbyterian Church. In introducing Blaine, Burchard labeled the Democrats the party of "Rum, Romanism, and Rebellion."

The alliterative slur not only waved the bloody shirt once again but fawned on anti-Catholics and the devotees of prohibition. Blaine, waiting to speak, may not even have attended to Burchard's remark, but the Democrats who were shadowing the Blaine forces caught it. Arthur Pue Gorman, chief architect of the Cleveland campaign, was overjoyed as he gave the order: "See to it that that statement is in every newspaper in the country by tomorrow." Instantly, Irish Catholic voters, clustered in New York, expressed outrage. Blaine, of course, repudiated Burchard's smart-alecky epigram and tried his best to distance himself from it, but the damage had been done. No one will ever know how many votes it changed.

October 29 was a double disaster for Blaine. That night a "prosperity dinner" was held for him at Delmonico's. The guest list of two hundred of America's richest men was a who's who of American capitalism. The men of power had rarely been seen together in such numbers. The carriages that brought them lined the streets of the neighborhood. Blaine in his address seemed fixed on money and truckled to the plutocrats, who roared their approval of him.

The following day the *New York World* ran a cartoon by Walt McDougall. Entitled "The Royal Feast of Belshazzar Blaine and the Money Kings," it presented caricatures of some of the diners at their banquet table, feasting on such delicacies as "Monopoly Soup," "Lobby Pudding," and "Navy Contract." In the foreground an impoverished couple clad in rags begged for a handout from them.

The lavish affair was simply out of place during a business turndown that had already cost so many jobs and added to so much poverty in the city, visible to any casual passerby only a few blocks from the scene of the event. The Blaine campaign had miscalculated: the money raising done at the affair could not cancel the effect on public opinion, particularly the opinion of working people who were already beginning to break their historic tie to the Republican Party.

On Election Day, Tuesday, November 4, Cleveland carried the Solid South, and Blaine found his strength in the Middle West. Heavy rains in the upstate counties of New York conspired against Blaine, keeping farmers and other likely supporters from the polls. The outcome was in dispute for several days, and a recount was ordered. How much skulduggery may have taken place is not knowable. Various witnesses were sure they had seen ballot boxes floating in the Hudson River, implying that some, maybe Republican, votes had not been counted. In the end, Cleveland carried the state and the election. The Republican domination of the presidency that began with Lincoln's election a quarter of a century earlier had come to an end. The joy of the Democrats knew no bounds, and the victory rallies for their man seemed endless. Now party members had a new chant:

Hurrah for Maria! Hurrah for the kid.
I voted for Cleveland. And damned glad I did.

The triumph in New York had given Cleveland 219 votes in the Electoral College—a squeaky 37 more votes than Blaine. Cleveland won the popular majority by 24,000 votes.

5

In the White House

In victory, Cleveland was magnanimous. Drowned in congratulatory messages, he wrote Bissell: "It's quite amusing to see how profuse the professions are of some of those who stood aloof when most needed. I intend to cultivate the Christian virtue of charity toward all men except the dirty class that defiled themselves with filthy scandal and Ballism. I don't believe God will ever forgive them and I am determined never to do so." At the same time, his mind was also fixed on what lay ahead. If he was apprehensive, one would not be surprised. The president-elect had never before set foot in Washington.

One can only wonder as to what people thought they had accomplished in putting Cleveland in office. He had no "program" except a commitment to honesty and efficiency and an intention to staff his administration with worthy people from the Democratic ranks. He told Bissell that he viewed the four years to come "as a dreadful self-afflicted penance for the good of my country. I see no pleasure in it and no satisfaction, only a hope that I may be of service." Since no man has ever been dragged against his will into service as president, it may be safely assumed that the "martyrdom" Cleveland was about to suffer was pose, not truly his sentiment. He believed that Divine Providence had made him president, and that fact laid upon him a

determination to conduct himself with a devotion to duty that
brooked no favors to anyone. Shortly after his election, while
strolling with a confidant, he put it this way: "Henceforth I must
have no friends."

Cleveland was not literally seeking "no friends"; he was simply
determined to form his administration from those he regarded
as the best men. If there was resentment among long-standing
associates he passed over, only a few were bold enough to tell
him. One of the rejected was Bissell, his boon companion, who
blistered the president-elect in private correspondence. Bissell
dearly wished a cabinet post, but by the time Cleveland got
around to considering him, no places were open: two New Yorkers had already been named. While Cleveland no doubt would
have liked to have had Bissell in Washington for company, and
could have given him a ceremonial post, the affronted friend
would have none of it. By way of defense, Cleveland relied self-
righteously on his old assurance to himself and those around
him that he was acting in the best interests of the public. If
people said he was "selfish and doubting my attachment to
them . . . I shall certainly be unhappy, but shall nevertheless
struggle on." Bissell eventually recovered from his pique, and in
Cleveland's second administration, which began eight years
later, he was in the cabinet.

Because there had not been a Democratic president for a
whole generation, talent for high office was hard to find. So
Cleveland had to seek out and personally recruit trustworthy
men of his own bent. They proved to be Bourbon Democracy
incarnate, figures closely identified with big business and railroad interests, whose names could not arouse editorial displea-
sure and who could keep a low profile in their new posts. While
they represented the East, West, and South adequately, they
included no spokesman for wage earners and farmers or for the
freedmen. Not a single party hack was in the lot, and no old-
time Jacksonians either, men still dreaming of a return to the
leveling democracy that the memory of "King Andrew" evoked.

Three of the posts went to northeasterners: the Department of State acquired Thomas F. Bayard, who had been a senator from Delaware for sixteen years and was reputed to have the best mind in public life. That he had been a presidential aspirant himself in 1884 made his appointment a generous gesture, reminding some people of how Lincoln had chosen a rival, William H. Seward, for state and Garfield more recently had named Blaine. Bayard carried himself with immense self-assurance, was not identified with the business world, favored free trade and sound money, and could be relied upon to ignore jingoism and the simmering zeal to join the competition for colonies.

Treasury got the party warhorse, Daniel Manning, Cleveland's longtime political guru. That appointment paid off Samuel Tilden, who had extracted a promise from Cleveland to put Manning in the cabinet in exchange for Tilden's endorsement of Cleveland's candidacy. Navy went to William C. Whitney, who had labored in the vineyards to make Cleveland the president, his contribution including a donation of twenty thousand dollars to the war chest. A rich man, he lived in the most elegant mansion in New York City, at Fifth Avenue and Fifty-seventh Street. Whitney had helped lead the fight against the Tweed Ring. He would have preferred a role behind the scenes, but he could not refuse what he was proffered. Only forty-three years old in 1885, Whitney was closely associated with the emerging urban streetcar industry, which in that day was as important as the telecommunication business in our time. He had served as corporation counsel of New York for seven years, and in that role had helped bring about the consolidation of the street-railway system of the city. He would have been a good fit in the Department of the Treasury, but he had acquired barnacles as a "tool of big business," and there were loud rumbles about that impression in the West, where the silver interests were having their say.

In the War Department, Cleveland placed William Crowninshield Endicott of Massachusetts, another conservative voice who served on his state's supreme court. He was a Harvard man and a former Whig who had not gone into the Republican Party in 1856. Instead, he became a Democrat and supported Buchanan. That, as an advocate of reform, he had good relations with the Republican Mugwumps made him especially attractive to an incoming administration.

In keeping with his determination to be a healer of the nation, Cleveland chose for his cabinet also two men from the former Confederacy: Lucius Q. C. Lamar of Mississippi as secretary of the interior and Augustus H. Garland of Arkansas as attorney general. Lamar had helped draft his state's ordnance of secession, and he had served for two years in the Confederate army. An able and learned man who had once taught mathematics, political economy, and law at the University of Mississippi, he was a favorite of his peers in the Senate. While he took second place to no one in defending white supremacy, he was no backward-glancing exponent of the old plantation tradition he had once defended so passionately. He was an advocate of the New South, envisioning there the growth of railroads and industry. In 1877 he had helped to engineer the compromise that ended the disputed presidential election of the previous year and made Rutherford B. Hayes the president.

Garland, a former governor of his state and now in his second term as senator, like Lamar, supported the new view that the South's future was bound up with the development of business. He had served in the House and Senate of the Confederacy, but now he too was hoping to create a new South on the ashes of the old. Cleveland acknowledged the West by appointing William F. Vilas of Wisconsin as postmaster general. Vilas was another younger figure—only forty-three years old. The leaders of the New York Democratic Party had recognized his ability as a lawyer and strategist. Cleveland had been impressed by his performance at the convention, and he took a strong liking to Vilas when he saw him with the committee that informed Cleveland of his nomination.

The newspapers were neither exalted nor disappointed by the cabinet selections. Cleveland, after all, was not an exciting and imaginative groundbreaker. He was doing what was expected of him, and that was all the reassurance that the people wanted. This was still a period of what was called "slack-water politics," a politics not marked by strong tides. The slavery question had been taken care of, the intense drama of the Civil War was past, and the reconstruction of the Union was by now regarded as complete.

Cleveland left Albany for Washington on March 2 aboard a special train. Accompanying him were some members of his family and Lamont and Manning. Lamont was to be his private secretary and "man Friday" as always, and would continue to address him as "Governor." In time, Lamont would give the position of private secretary to the president an importance it had not previously had. Cleveland had insisted on paying the train fare, rejecting the offer from the railroad of a free trip. He also turned down an invitation from outgoing President Arthur to stay at the White House. Instead, he took rooms at the Arlington Hotel nearby. Shortly after arriving, Cleveland went to the White House to pay his respects to Arthur, who spent an hour showing him around the mansion. The next day Arthur returned the courtesy call at the Arlington.

March 4 was beautiful and sunny, one of the warmest Inauguration Days Washington has known. Pennsylvania Avenue was alive with flowers and garlands hanging from many windows along the route. The throng of spectators, many attired in Sunday best, seemed bursting to cheer the new president when he appeared. Accompanied only by a military unit, Cleveland and Arthur rode side by side to the Capitol in a White House barouche drawn by four handsome bay horses. When Cleveland came into sight on the East Portico and entered the specially erected platform, the assemblage went wild with delight. He ignored the thunderous ovation, almost as if he had not heard it, and sat down, chatting affably with Arthur next to him. At a little after one o'clock, Cleveland rose, and amid more cheering, he silenced the crowed as he began his inaugural address from memory, startling the audience with such boldness. Most people did not know that Cleveland, who almost invariably spoke without notes in the courtroom and in his public addresses, was well practiced in the art of memorized oratory. Not everyone was impressed by his physical appearance. Robert M. La Follette, a new member of the House from Wisconsin, who was destined to have his own role in presidential politics, contrasted Cleveland unkindly with the handsome Chester Arthur: "Cleveland's coarse face, his heavy inert body, his great shapeless hands, confirmed in my mind the attacks made upon him during the campaign."

The address, lasting only about fifteen minutes, was, except for its mode of delivery, undistinguished. The new president paid his respects to the change of party: "To-day the executive branch of the government is transferred to new keeping. . . . At this hour the animosities of political strife, the bitterness of partisan defeat, and the exultation of partisan triumph should be supplanted by an ungrudging acquiescence in the popular will. . . ." He urged that those in public office "limit public expenditures to the actual needs of the government economically administered." He promised reform in the management of government "and the application of business principles to public affairs." He called for fair and honest treatment of the Indians, condemned polygamy in the territories, and, in a deep bow to labor, rigorous enforcement of the immigration laws so as to exclude "a servile class [natives of China] to compete with American labor, with no intention of acquiring citizenship, and bringing with them and retaining habits and customs repugnant to our civilization." In foreign affairs he pledged himself to the policy of the Founding Fathers: "Peace, commerce, and honest friendship with all nations: entangling alliances with none."

Cleveland had insisted on reversing the usual order of the ceremony, so that he was sworn in after, not before, the inaugural address. He hoped thereby to emphasize in his own fashion the solemn significance of the occasion, declaring in his opening sentence: "I am about to supplement and seal by the oath which I shall take the manifestation and will of a great and free people." Chief Justice Morrison R. Waite, only recently confirmed in his post, administered the oath on the president's beloved Bible.

Throughout his term, Cleveland would keep the book in a drawer of the handsome double-pedestal desk that Queen Victoria had recently presented to the United States. She had sent it in appreciation of American efforts to discover the whereabouts of the expedition led by Sir John Franklin, the Arctic explorer lost in the late 1840s while seeking the Northwest Passage. Cleveland could not but have been told the history of the elegant gift: Franklin's ship, HMS *Resolute*, had been found crushed in the ice by an American ship captain. Rebuilt and returned to England, it was put back into service. When it was finally decommissioned and dismantled, some of its oak timbers were fashioned into this unique present delivered to President Hayes. Known in the White House today as the "*Resolute* desk," it served many presidents in the family quarters of the White House. President Kennedy moved it into the Oval Office where he and successors continued to enjoy its use.

When the inauguration ceremony was finished, the president and the ex-president entered their carriage again for the ride back to the White House, where Cleveland reviewed the seemingly endless parade in his honor. At its conclusion he had a much-delayed lunch with Arthur, who left for New York immediately afterward. The Cleveland era—and few could have guessed how long it would be—was about to begin.

That evening a feature of the ball in the Pension Building was the presence of John Philip Sousa's United States Marine Band, already called "the President's own." The dramatic redbrick edifice in which the celebration was held—today the National Building Museum—was still under construction. Located in Downtown East, it had been erected solely to house the Pension Bureau and to serve the needs of Union army veterans. Cleveland's use of it for his inauguration ball, though, began a tradition that continues to the present day of holding presidential festivities in its majestic Great Hall.

Even as the evening unfolded, Cleveland's mind was on the morrow, for before the very day was done he was being assailed by office seekers. He had not yet settled in at the White House— a daunting task in itself, because there was insufficient staff to assist. In the oval room on the second floor was his office. He had one telephone on which all the business of the nation had to be conducted, and no stenographer. His most important help- mate was the faithful William Sinclair, his valet and jack-of-all- trades.

The public knew that their new president lived a spartan existence, but that he indulged one pleasure—eating, which anybody could see. The meals prepared for him were elaborate, although unless he was entertaining guests no wine was served. Sometimes the fare struck him as too fancy. He did not enjoy the offerings of the French chef he had inherited from the urbane Chester Arthur. Cleveland would write to Bissell: "I must go to dinner, but I wish it was to eat pickled herring, Swiss cheese and a chop at Louis' instead of the French stuff I shall find." Once, as his supper was being presented, he smelled the appetizing aroma of corned beef and cabbage coming from the servant quarters. To the dismay of the chef, he said to Sinclair, "Well, William, take this dinner down to the servants and bring their dinner to me." He declared it the best food he had had for months.

In keeping with his practice in every public office he held, he went over the accounts of the White House and made out per- sonal checks for expenses incurred that were not official ones. The loneliness of life in the White House seems not to have fazed him, nor did his elegant surroundings awe him. The mail, which took up most of his time, was effectively winnowed by the able Dan Lamont, who knew the president's mind as well as his own. Cleveland, as he had as mayor and then as governor, worked incessantly. Unlike other men of affairs, he conducted his business until well into the night, sitting only a few yards from his bedroom. Arising each morning at six, he was back at his desk by eight o'clock in the winter and even earlier in the summer. Occasionally he took time off to go fishing, but he refused to use the *Dispatch*, the yacht available to presidents.

His maiden sister, Rose, served as his official hostess. She was a feminist ahead of her time, with ideas far in advance of those held by her brother. A full-bodied woman who carried herself mannishly, she hated the receiving lines she had to endure, and reported that to relieve her boredom, she recited to herself the conjugations of Greek verbs. Her book, *George Eliot's Poetry and Other Studies*, had just appeared, and her prominent position made it a best-seller, but she knew and said that it was not a work of general interest. She had struck many people as a scold when she condemned "the immodest dress of some few society women."

Seeking additional company, Cleveland invited the Lamonts to move into the White House with him for a while. Not only did he enjoy their conversation but he was also fond of their two little girls, whom he sometimes took to the fountain on the south lawn to watch them feed the goldfish.

Mostly, Cleveland was all business. He had, though, not given up his interest in baseball, and he followed the team standings as best he could. Once, in his first year in office, when the Chicago White Stockings were in town for a game, he invited the team to the White House. He took the occasion to ask Cap Anson, the player-manager: "How's my old friend 'Pud' Galvin [once the star pitcher for the Buffalo Bisons and now a Hall of Famer]? You know he and I were good friends when I was sheriff and mayor of Buffalo." But when Anson invited the president to the ballpark, Cleveland felt he had to say "no thank you." "What do you think the American people would think of me if I wasted my time going to a ball game?"

Cleveland kept himself accessible to officeholders and the people alike. He received in the morning (beginning at ten every day except Sunday and Monday) for anyone with business to see him about. Monday he reserved for consultation with cabinet officers. Meetings of the whole cabinet were held on Tuesday and Thursday at noon; his official family served as a sounding board for policies, an arrangement that would soon be obsolete in the White House. He continued to abhor public dinners because he was not good at after-dinner speaking, which required a lighter language and a readier wit than he could provide—although he did not entirely lack a sense of humor. Close friends said he could tell a joke well, and that he was an amusing mimic of other politicians. The plain truth was that Cleveland had no gift for public relations.

Moreover, his disdain for the press—always strong but no doubt reinforced by the treatment he had received during the campaign—was unqualified. He was the last president who refused to give working space to reporters. They were forced to stand outside the White House in all kinds of weather and be content with interviewing visitors as they entered or left. And when pressed to name a new private secretary who would be more forthcoming to journalists, Cleveland's response was clear: "I have a notion to appoint a man who will be good to me." Cleveland remains the only president who refused to attend the annual dinner of the Gridiron Club, the insider association of Washington journalists founded in 1885, at which the president and the press attired in white tie and tails "singe but do not burn" each other with more or less good-natured sallies.

Cleveland's stern character showed itself in his resistance to fellow Democrats who worked to oust Republicans from government jobs. Those who importuned him soon discovered that he meant what he had said, that the day of the spoilsmen was over. There were moments when he felt overwhelmed by the pressures of job seekers—even as his predecessors in the presidency had been. Still, he wrote a friend: "I wake at night in the White House and rub my eyes and wonder if it is all a dream."

The integrity of the men chosen for the cabinet was impressive. Although the members were conservatives with little desire to change things, they served the people as Cleveland wished. For instance, Postmaster General Vilas, although linked to railroad interests, went after the lines with zeal when he found them overcharging the government for hauling the mail. Unsuccessful in his efforts, he decided to seek from Congress government ownership of the mail cars and authority to operate them. In the end he failed, and it was not until Woodrow Wilson's day, thirty years later, that Vilas's proposal was made into law.

Although Cleveland was essentially an isolationist and uninterested in military and naval affairs, he was keen for the expansion of the navy that was the aim of William C. Whitney. Whitney encouraged the nation's steel manufacturers to produce the sheet steel required for building warships and thus eliminate dependence on foreign sources. The great powers of Europe had already entered the age of overseas imperialism. But Cleveland was not tempted. He supported a modernized navy because he saw it as a defender of America's coastlines.

In the Interior Department, Lamar was employed in reordering what remained of the frontier. Railroad men, land companies, and cattle barons had taken great liberties and often committed fraud in turning the public domain to selfish use. Barbed wire had enclosed many thousands of acres illegally, denying them to legitimate settlers and often elbowing out Indian tribes that had a right to their use. It was Cleveland's purpose to liberate also millions of acres that the railroads had acquired, and open them to development by legitimate settlers.

As with the building of the new navy, Cleveland's politics— sometimes more insistent than Lamar wanted or that Attorney General Garland recommended—laid the groundwork for changes that would afterward be associated with the rise of Progressivism. Vilas was one of the heroes of the administration, a pioneer whose name and fame have been largely forgotten. When Lamar was appointed to the Supreme Court in 1887, Vilas took his place at Interior. His impulses as a westerner showed quickly when he turned his energy to helping the lumber interests obtain access to forest land occupied by Indians in Wisconsin. Although querulous eyes were raised in Congress, investigation showed no fraud. This was a businessman's administration, and material progress was a legitimate goal. Moreover, the Indians were beneficiaries of the increasing prosperity that (it was said) they shared in. It had not yet become the business of government to interfere with the natural laws of the economy.

In his first summer, Cleveland broke away from the White House and, after attending General Grant's funeral in New York, headed with a claque of friends for the Adirondacks to hunt and fish and play cards. His weight was now so great—possibly nearly three hundred pounds—that he could not keep up with his cronies on the hunt, and he mainly fished and ate. Clearly, he needed companionship. The following spring, rumors were afoot that the president was contemplating marriage. Cleveland, in line with his general hostility to the press, refused to confirm or deny the report. But it was long known to Cleveland's close associates that in 1875, in the course of managing the estate of his late law partner Oscar Folsom, he had grown close to Mrs. Folsom, the widow, and to their daughter, Frances, then eleven years old. He became virtually her guardian. She knew him as "Uncle Cleve." Her name was actually Frank, because she had been named for an uncle, and that was how Cleveland always addressed her. She took the name Frances as she grew up, regarding it as more proper for a woman. In time the newspaper people would refer to her as "Frankie," an appellation she detested.

Cleveland's relationship with the Folsoms was so intimate that the gossipmongers were not sure whether his close friend was the widow or the daughter. While Frank was at Wells College in Aurora, New York, Cleveland obtained the mother's permission to correspond with her. In 1885 Cleveland and the pretty, spirited young woman became betrothed. The engagement had followed a series of letter exchanges in which the president proposed marriage. But mum was the word to the public. When the *Cincinnati Enquirer* asked Cleveland directly if he was engaged, he retorted: "I am not going to say a word in the matter, but let you go on in your own way until you get tired of dragging the name of the poor, defenseless girl into cruel publicity." Few can doubt that the bachelor president, now past his forty-eighth birthday, felt some embarrassment in courting a woman almost twenty-seven years his junior.

As a graduation present, Frank toured Europe in the late spring of 1886 with her mother and a cousin. Already plans had been laid for a June wedding. On May 27 the Folsoms arrived back in New York aboard a United States revenue cutter, having been transferred from their ship, the *Noordland*. They were met by Lamont and Rose Cleveland, who took the women to Gilsey House, where the wives of the cabinet members waited to receive them. The Folsoms were considerably distressed by the news they had received aboard their boat that Frank's grandfather, John Folsom, had died. This cast a pall over the wedding plans, for it was in his house that the pair had expected to be married. Since Cleveland ruled out a church wedding and would not entertain the idea of a hotel, the White House was to be the site. To his cabinet at its regular Thursday morning meeting on May 27, Cleveland finally confirmed the gossip about impending nuptials. Being uncomfortable with social niceties, as we have seen, he relied on the advice of his married sister Mary for the details of what would be the first wedding of a president ever held in the White House.

The scheduled wedding day, June 2, saw the Blue Room as no one had ever seen it before: it was fairly covered from floor to ceiling with bowers of spring blossoms. The makeshift altar was illuminated by white candles in two giant candelabra that had been a gift of President Jackson to the White House. All the cabinet members and their wives were in their places, save Garland, who had declined the invitation in tribute to the memory of his deceased wife: he had vowed never again to attend a festive gathering. A few relatives and friends filled the remainder of the seats—thirty-one guests in all.

Promptly at seven o'clock, the bridal couple came down the aisle to the wedding march played by the United States Marine Band, Sousa conducting. The bride, radiant in a dress brought from Europe of corded ivory satin with a fifteen-foot train, was naturally the centerpiece of the event. All eyes were fixed on the first lady to be. (Cleveland would always prefer the designation "the President's lady.") The simple Presbyterian service was performed by the president's pastor in Washington, the Reverend Byron Sunderland. In words notably the work of Cleveland, Frank pledged "to love . . . honor, comfort, and keep" her groom, a remarkable emendation to tradition that was duly remarked upon in the press. At the conclusion of the ceremony the president's brother, the Reverend William, offered a blessing.

A reception and a light supper in the State Dining Room followed. There, congratulatory messages were read aloud, including one from Queen Victoria. The Clevelands had received a mountain of gifts, and especially from the wealthier cabinet officers handsome diamond jewelry, but the only item on display was a diamond necklace, Cleveland's gift to his beloved. The newlyweds slipped away in the middle of the evening and took a train to their honeymoon retreat at Deer Park, in western Maryland.

The president had rented a cottage there nestled in the woods on land facing the Blue Ridge Mountains then at the height of their springtime beauty—though it was raining when the bridal couple arrived. Choosing this site proved a mistake. The hounds of the media had discovered the location, and the next morning, as Cleveland emerged from the cabin, he found himself facing what one newspaper called "the flower of Washington journalism." He was furious at what he called this "colossal impertinence." Still, he was helpless to change what was now a public clamor for tidbits about people in high position. How different had been the experience of President John Tyler forty-two years earlier. Then Tyler had married a prominent beauty thirty years younger than he in a church in New York City, no less, and the event was a solemn secret. Now, for the first time a president's personal life had been invaded by prying newsmen, thereby opening a window on the presidency and the president's privacy that has never been closed again. The press would not be denied its access and would eventually argue that the right to know was an inalienable right they must defend.

The marriage had a salutary effect on Cleveland's standing with the public. Frances Cleveland was a golden asset, because she conducted herself with uncommon aplomb and propriety. She decorated the White House with flowers, and she made her canaries and her Japanese poodle and various other breeds of dog welcome additions to daily life. A leading Republican predicted that Cleveland would now be a more formidable candidate in the next election: "It will be much harder to win against both Mr. and Mrs. Cleveland." Although the first lady gave no interviews, she had a gift for dealing with people that astonished the president, himself so conspicuously awkward in personal comportment. Frances held two receptions a week, one of them on Saturdays, so that young women, now increasingly important in the Washington labor force, could attend. Sometimes she greeted as many as eight thousand people. Whenever she appeared in public, she provoked a mob scene of curious people bent on catching a glimpse of her.

Cleveland was acutely aware that the White House was unsatisfactory for proper family life. The amount of household help was inadequate. Indeed, sometimes the president himself felt forced to answer a knock on the front door. So, shortly before his wedding, Cleveland had bought a country house not far from the White House, just outside the limits of the District of Columbia, on what is now Wisconsin Avenue, known as Cleveland Park. Remodeled and refurnished, the retreat served as a weekend place for the presidential couple. It had a commanding view of the Potomac and the whole of official Washington. Frances Cleveland liked to call it Oak View, but Cleveland had the roof painted red—and the ever-vigilant press corps referred to it as Red Top.

The first lady enjoyed her role as hostess of the White House, and as the administration grew older, social life became livelier. Moreover, the president had been softened in the public's regard

by leaving the bachelor state. Beneath his starched exterior
there had always been a sympathetic heart, and people became
aware of his gentler qualities. He gave them expression not in
his formal speeches, which were invariably dry and dull, as we
have seen, but in the well-turned letters that he composed. Still,
his frequent outburst of temper, his brusque treatment of defi-
cient subordinates, and what was sometimes plain grossness
were also in notable evidence. These traits bespoke an unalter-
able gracelessness that people took as a small price to pay for the
honesty in government he had brought with him They understood he meant what everybody said he believed: "A public
office is a public trust."

In conducting the business of the presidency, Cleveland
found himself caught up in the continuing problem of filling
jobs in the expanding federal bureaucracy. He spent endless
hours going over applications, sometimes sitting for hours,
for instance, with Vilas, trusting that they could make proper
choices in filling the ranks of postmasters around the country.

At first the civil service reformers who had supported him so
enthusiastically and so hopefully were delighted with his work.
He even appointed some Republicans to significant positions,
especially in New York and Massachusetts, where reform sentiment was strong. He pleased immensely the good government
people—including influential Mugwumps like Godkin of *The
Nation*, Carl Schurz, the beloved German immigrant and friend
of Lincoln who was now senator from Missouri, and members
of the National Civil Service Reform League. In their best
moments, men of this stamp imagined that Cleveland would
appoint on merit alone and that half of the appointees would be
Democrats and half would be Republican! But the pressure
from the regular Democrats was also intense: their party had
been out of office for so long that their thirst for jobs was
unquenchable. Cleveland was beside himself as he dealt with
the competing demands, exclaiming at one time: "My God, what
is there in this office that any man should ever want to get
into it!"

In the end, the fate of the Democratic Party weighed more heavily on the president than the call of reform. To the dismay of the reformers, particularly the Mugwumps, Cleveland's actions resulted in the dismissal of thousands of jobholders, simply in order to replace them with Democrats. The reformers stayed on the case. The Civil Service Reform League insisted that the president give an explanation for every change in officeholder he made. Of course, Cleveland would countenance no such arrangement. Yet he was sensitive to their deep disappointment, and he was able to satisfy himself that he had made fewer changes in personnel than Republican predecessors.

Another issue that Cleveland wrestled with was the legacy of the Civil War. It took several forms. Although two decades had passed since Appomattox, like Vietnam a century later, it remained in national politics a boil that could not be lanced. In every town, north and south, armless sleeves and legless trousers were daily visual reminders of the appalling carnage that had convulsed the nation. Everywhere—in the plight of the freed slaves, in the economic decline of the South, in the increasing infirmities of Union army veterans—there was need for help. But nobody yet was saying that it was the duty of the federal government to provide its people with welfare relief. Although reconciliation between the sections was well under way, and the Union had been restored, people could see how much remained to be done.

Trouble for the administration developed from the pension fever then plaguing Congress. A bill was introduced on the Hill to give a pension to any Union army veteran who had served at least ninety days. Cleveland vetoed the proposal as a raid on the public treasury. The veto brought Cleveland intense opprobrium from Republicans, though not from the business community. It did not lessen his support in the South, where there were only Confederate veterans who would not benefit from federal pensions.

Without hesitation, Cleveland forcefully and defiantly vetoed also the pension bills that members of Congress were introducing on behalf of favored veterans in their home districts. The

justification offered was often both laughable and sad. One family, for instance, sought a pension for the service of a son who
had drowned in a canal—after deserting from the army. While
many former soldiers agreed with the president's stand, others
among them were provoked, particularly because Cleveland
himself had not served. There were, indeed, legitimate objections to Cleveland's actions. For example, in filling federal
offices, he had given preference only to disabled veterans, not to
all veterans, which a more just system should have provided for.
Moreover, his veto messages were often accompanied by sarcas-
tic language.

The president angered veterans further when he went fishing
on Decoration Day. But nothing aroused Union veterans more
than his action in ordering the return to the states of captured
Civil War flags and banners. The decision was a miscalculation,
although it was taken without premeditation. Apparently, the
idea of doing this as a gesture to the former Confederacy came
from Endicott, the well-meaning but naïve secretary of war.
Cleveland, in a typically routine way, assented orally. The outcry
was fierce. Running for reelection to the Senate in Ohio, for
instance, Joseph B. Foraker made of the administration's action a
campaign issue: the Democrats, he declared, were attempting to
reestablish the Confederacy. The commander of the G.A.R.,
Lucius Fairchild, a hero-general of the Battle of Gettysburg,
excoriated the president at a rally in New York: "May God palsy
the hand that wrote that order. May God palsy the brain that
conceived it; and may God palsy the tongue that dictated it."

It hardly mitigated the effects of the president's misstep that
some of the newspapers in the country ridiculed the general as
"Fairchild of the Three Palsies." Eager to see the North and
South fully united again, Cleveland lacked the diplomacy, the
"touch" to bring it about. His plainspoken honesty, such an
important part of his makeup, also made him often blind and
deaf to public sentiment. On a tour of the West, despite urging
from his associates, he refused to disrupt his schedule to go to
Springfield, Illinois, to pay his respects at Lincoln's tomb. While

visiting the battlefield at Gettysburg, he declined to make even a brief speech, likely believing that Lincoln had spoken all that had to be said there. And toward the freedmen, prime products of the war, he made no gesture of support and offered no helping hand.

In Cleveland's view, the president was simply what the Constitution said he was, the chief executive, a referee making sure that no individual or group is granted special favors or deprived of their rights. In this regard he was not different from many of his predecessors. Nevertheless, new issues were arising, and an assertive public opinion, made more animated by the coming of the modern media, would change the scene.

Cleveland did not see any of this as altering his proud office. He vetoed a bill that would have provided assistance to Texas farmers largely wiped out by a severe drought. In his accompanying message he declared in words that seemed ordinary but that would be unacceptable today: "I do not believe that the power and duty of the general government ought to be extended to the relief of individual suffering which is in no manner properly related to the public service or benefit." He stated a principle: "Though the people support the government, the government should not support the people."

Still, Cleveland did not shrink from other kinds of intervention in economic activity. He was pleased to sign into law the Interstate Commerce Act to regulate railroad rates. The law provided for the creation of an Interstate Commerce Commission—the first of a long series of regulatory agencies that would involve the federal government directly in the lives of individuals. Moreover, Cleveland was determined to deal with the tariff, a lively issue of the day, because people in every section of the country believed that rates were excessively high. They made the argument that the duties enriched manufacturers at the expense of consumers and produced an unnecessary surplus in the federal Treasury besides. In 1886–87, the surplus was $103 million, and an even larger one was anticipated for the next fiscal year.

Cleveland had not quickly reached the conclusion that the tariff was the culprit in the economy. Before he became president it is doubtful that he had thought about the subject at all. But his cabinet consisted of railroad and finance men who were low-tariff advocates, and his closest friends, including now Vilas, were in that camp. In September 1887 the president had hosted a gathering of political leaders at Oak View, a meeting that included Speaker of the House John G. Carlisle and the new secretary of the Treasury, Charles S. Fairchild, who had replaced Manning when Manning fell ill earlier in the year. Out of the Oak View conference came plans for a bill to lower the tariff. Cleveland had become a confirmed convert to the cause, and, as a candidate for reelection in '88, he was determined to be the leading activist in behalf of party policy.

On December 6, in an unheard-of initiative to dramatize the urgency he felt the subject deserved, he devoted his entire third annual message to it. (Since World War II, this yearly presidential deliverance has been called the state of the union message.) Cleveland called upon Congress to reduce the rates as soon as possible. He had vetted the text beforehand with his cabinet. Not all of the members were pleased with its strong tone or the singleness of the subject. Whitney, especially, was anxious about Cleveland's determination to deliver it, pleading that the action would cost the party New York in the forthcoming election.

Cleveland would not be dissuaded. His language made Republicans and protectionist Democrats furious, many vowing political revenge. Cleveland's words were potent in the time-honored way that presidents and the people's representatives confront one another: "If disaster results from the inaction of Congress, the responsibility must rest where it belongs." He did not propose tariff rates so low that they "imperiled the existence of our manufacturing interests. But this existence should not mean a condition which, without regard to the public welfare or a national exigency, must always insure the realization of immense profits instead of moderately profitable returns." And he added, in mollifying the factory owners, that a reduced tariff would make raw materials cheaper, thus compensating for the reduction in the price they charged for finished products. Furthermore, cheaper goods would open wider foreign markets for manufacturers, "saving them from the depression, interruption in business, and loss caused by a glutted domestic market and affording their employees more certain and steady labor, with its resulting quiet and contentment." Along with his approval of the new Interstate Commerce Commission, Cleveland had done his bit to serve the business community despite some grumbling from it. He thought it ought to be satisfied with the administration. The rising voice of farm organizations and the calls for action against monopolies expressed by such writers as Henry George and Henry Demarest Lloyd were not within Cleveland's hearing. The president was fixated on the tariff.

In general, the newspaper editors applauded the message. The *New York Commercial Advertiser* characterized it as "concise, able and manfully candid." Most people, however, were ignorant of the subject and its ramifications, if they knew at all that it was being debated. The tariff was for the informed to worry about and the politicians to make political hay of. Many Democrats were sure that Cleveland had cooked his goose and theirs too by his single-minded stubbornness; the Republicans were confident they would soon be back in the White House. Senator Blaine assailed the message as a plea for "free trade," a doctrine that to him sounded wrong because it was also British policy. Republicans also expected to have the vote of industrial workers who were being told that the tariff was a bulwark of high wages, and a necessary barrier against the "pauper labor" of Europe. This view fitted with the belief of laboring men in that era that it was in their interest generally to vote as their employers did.

In the midterm election in 1886, the Democrats had held their own: they still controlled the House, although they had lost fourteen seats, and they had narrowed to a sliver the Republican control of the Senate. For the first time since 1840 a Democratic president running for reelection would be obliged to defend his record before the public.

Cleveland, alas, had always been a passive commander, and holding the presidency had not changed his natural inclination. He had come out of the gate strong for tariff reform, but he did not crusade for it—evidencing once again that he was not a fighter. On the Hill, the tariff proposal, known as the Mills bill, after Representative Roger Q. Mills of Texas, chairman of the Ways and Means Committee, had so many hands laid on it that it dropped the average level of the tariff on imports only from 47 percent to 40 percent. It passed the House but died in committee in the Senate. The result was not what Cleveland had hoped for, but the country at last had an issue that distinguished the two major parties from each other and, for the first time in a long generation, an issue of some substance.

Practically unmentioned throughout the 1886 campaign was the growing disparity between the rich and the poor. A massacre at Haymarket Square in Chicago on May 4, 1886, had dramatized the issue for the first time for millions of Americans. After the police had broken up a meeting of anarcho-communists, a bomb was exploded in the ranks of the police, killing seven officers and wounding many more. The culprit responsible was never identified. Property owners were terrified by the event, seeing it as a portent of violence to come. Cleveland was already attuned to the growing tension between labor and capital: the previous month he had sent a special message to Congress on the subject, the first such ever transmitted from the White House. He called for legislation "providing for the arbitration of disputes between laboring men and employers." He proposed as an adjunct to the Bureau of Labor the establishment of a Commission of Labor to be "charged among other duties with the consideration and settlement, when possible, of all controversies between labor and capital." In his annual message in December that year he repeated his call for such an arrangement.

But Cleveland did not press Congress, and the proposition was never acted upon. Although the condition of the laboring man remained on his mind—on a visit to Chicago he asked to be taken to Haymarket Square to view the site of the tragedy—he shrank from crusading for ameliorative measures. The tariff would provide sufficient fodder for the battle ahead.

_____

6

Defeated for Reelection

The presidential campaign just getting under way was only of modest concern in most parts of the country, because the presidency was not yet the center of public attention. Although the Associated Press had been created in 1848 during President James K. Polk's administration, its dispatches still did not reach every journal. And to most citizens, the presidents after Lincoln seemed one like the other, marching across the years in lockstep. A renowned journalist, sharply critical of their performance, described the post–Civil War chief executives as "masks in a pageant."

To be sure, President Cleveland was respected wherever he went, but often he was exploited in a way that would be impermissible today. Pictures of him, and often Frances Cleveland with him, were turning up with increasing frequency on "trade cards" puffing every manner of consumer goods, from tobacco to matches, from soap to yard goods, from underwear to a "proven" cure for croup—as if the presidential couple were endorsing these products. Through such pieces of sales promotion, some Americans were enabled at least to attach a face to the notion of president and first lady. Even so, the gravitas of the White House was diminished in the process. Along with many other people, Henry James, the novelist, intuited this decline. In his short story

"Pandora," published in 1886, he has a character, a Mrs. Bonny-castle, one of the great givers of parties in Washington, whose husband says, "Hang it, there's only a month left [to the social season]. Let us be vulgar and have some fun—let us invite the President."

The canvass of 1888 was destined to be one in which the old tradition of name-calling and vituperation became blended with new techniques. For sale, but usually free, were beribboned badges, banners big enough to span a street, lapel buttons of many shapes and sizes, ceramic figurines of the principals, and engraved goblets touting the parties. But the ballyhoo could not hide the lackluster image of the candidates.

Meeting in St. Louis, in the Exposition Building, on June 5, the Democrats concluded their business in three days: the renomination of Cleveland was a foregone conclusion. The Tammany forces would have been more than willing to replace him, but they had no support. The president had all 822 ballots of the convention and was declared the candidate by acclamation. Allen Granberry Thurman, beloved as "The Old Roman," was named his running mate, although he had opposed Cleveland's positions on the tariff and on other issues. The president, aware of Thurman's personal popularity, raised no objections. The platform in tame, potato-in-the-mouth language endorsed "the view expressed by the President in his last message."

The president himself was lukewarm for a campaign or even for another term. He wrote to Bissell words that would be unimaginable from a nominee today: "I sometimes think that perhaps more enthusiasm would have been created if somebody else had been nominated after a lively scrimmage at St. Louis." Declaring he was "too busy" to go out on the hustings, Cleveland even ducked an important meeting with a national farmer group, maintaining that his attendance there would interfere with his vacation. Thurman, now seventy-five years old, carried on such campaigning as the ticket managed to exhibit. Ailing, and barely able to walk, he nevertheless worked hard. He was known for mopping his brow with a red bandanna, which inspired a popular song sold by the Democrats. It ended with the lines:

The Red Bandanna will elect two honest men I
*   know,*
The noblest Roman of them all and the Man from
*   Buffalo.*

The Republican Party gathered in Chicago in the Civic Audi-
torium on June 19. Blaine, then traveling in Italy, gave an inter-
view in Florence effectively taking himself out of the contest.
He said that having once had the honor of leading his party in a
presidential campaign and having been defeated, he owed fellow Republicans the courtesy of not seeking the nomination
again. Familiar names were on tap to be his successor. The leading ones were John Sherman of Ohio, brother of William Tecumseh Sherman, a veteran of the currency wars, who had served
brilliantly in the Senate and had been secretary of the Treasury
under President Hayes; Walter Q. Gresham of Indiana, a former
Whig who had helped organize the Republican Party and had
served as postmaster general and then secretary of the Treasury
under President Arthur; and Chauncey M. Depew of New York,
a manager of Cornelius Vanderbilt's railroad empire, and one of
the most sought-after banquet speakers of his day.

Another man in the running was Benjamin Harrison, also of
Indiana. He had an unmatched pedigree: his great-grandfather,
also Benjamin Harrison, had signed the Declaration of Independence for Virginia, a grandfather, William Henry Harrison, had
been president, and his father had been a two-term member of
Congress. Harrison had an enviable Civil War record. Knowing
nothing about war and its conduct, he had grown quickly into a
magnificent leader of the 70th Infantry, the volunteer brigade he
helped to raise. It performed impressively in the titanic struggle
for Atlanta in 1864. At the war's end Harrison was brevetted a
brigadier general. Back home, by dint of hard work, he had risen
to the top of the Indiana bar and become a fixture in the leadership of the Republican Party in Indiana. Still, his elective experience was thin: he had lost a race for governor, and recently after
serving a term in the Senate had been defeated for reelection.

Sherman led on the first ballot with 229 votes, needing only 187 more to win. Harrison, in fourth place and regarded as a "dark horse," was practically nowhere with 85 votes. Nevertheless, he seemed to be the most available man, carrying fewer political liabilities than the rest. His support grew with each succeeding roll call, and the delegates took him on at the eighth ballot. For vice president, the party chose Levi P. Morton of New York, one of the richest men in America. The Republican platform, hurling down the gauntlet to the Democrats, spoke out for a protective tariff and pledged generous pensions for veterans.

Harrison had long been derided by many Democrats as "Kid Glove Harrison" because he was something of a dandy and an unbending little man. Only five feet six inches tall, he invariably wore a beaver high hat, which became his emblem—it was modish, and it added to his height. Where the Democrats sang: "His Grandfather's Hat—It's Too Big for Ben," the Republicans rejoined: "The Same Old Hat—It Fits Ben Just Right." Still, nothing could make him a popular figure. Even colleagues regarded him as being "cold as an iceberg." Tom Platt once declared him to be "as glacial as a Siberian stripped of his fur."

The Republicans raised a campaign chest by coercing manufacturers into contributing if they wished to have tariff protection. Harrison's campaign chairman, Matt Quay of Pennsylvania, who had recently become a senator, said he was going to put those industrialists "under the fire and fry all the fat out of them." In New York the party raised four million dollars, an unheard-of sum. In addition to denouncing Cleveland as a "free trade" man, the Harrison forces were bent on hammering away at what the president had done about the Confederate battle flags. There is evidence that on Election Day some of the party faithful passed out money, even in the candidate's home state of Indiana, to buy the votes deemed necessary. They were said to cost as much as twenty dollars apiece.

Whereas Cleveland in 1884 had had to face the humiliation of his liaison with Maria Halpin, he now had to endure the rumor that in a drunken rage he had beaten his wife. He suffered yet another blow in the so-called Murchison affair. The facts are simple: a California Republican, using the false name of Charles F. Murchison, and posing as a British immigrant, had written to the British minister to the United States asking how he should vote in the election. The minister, Sir Lionel Sackville-West, then engaged in negotiations with the administration toward settling the long-festering question of the Canadian fisheries, fell into the trap. He suggested to "Murchison" that he vote for Cleveland. When this ill-considered and inappropriate reply was published two weeks before Election Day, it created a sensation. It conveyed the impression that Cleveland was in the hands of the British free traders and that England had a special interest in his reelection.

The modern campaign, with candidates traveling up and down the country, was only slowly emerging. But surrogates were in full supply. It is said that the money in the Republican pot made it possible for them to have ten times as many speakers on the stump as the Democrats. Sherman loyally toured swing states in the East, and Blaine gallantly put his prestige to work in New York and Indiana. New York drew special attention: the Republicans viewed it as ripe for the picking, the Democrats there being sharply divided. Cleveland's successor as governor, David B. Hill, was running for reelection, and since he thought he needed the backing of Tammany, Cleveland, and other reform-minded people, gave him only tepid support.

The Democrats had indeed some resourceful leaders. And Frances Cleveland was a choice asset. Her likeness appeared, sometimes without the president's, on millions of pieces of giveaways—handkerchiefs, scarves, pitchers, napkins, and bric-a-brac of every kind. Although feeling that much of this fanfare was beneath the dignity of the presidency, the Clevelands were powerless to halt its flow.

On Election Day, the country produced the closest result in American history. Cleveland had a plurality of slightly more than a hundred thousand popular votes—sources vary on the exact number. But Harrison carried the electoral college 233 to

168, having taken New York and Indiana, which Cleveland had won narrowly four years earlier. The White House was again in Republican hands.

Cleveland was never willing to denounce Hill, his former lieutenant governor, for treachery in not getting out the Democratic loyalists. When asked to explain the disappointing result, Cleveland wryly said: "It was mainly because the other party had the most votes." He insisted he was glad he had not yielded on his commitment to a lower tariff. He confessed to an acquaintance: "Perhaps I made a mistake from the party standpoint; but damn it, it was right." In truth, his loss of the election was a result not so much of his principled stand on the tariff but of a disjointed campaign and its lifeless leadership, including his own.

The devout Harrison declared in the aftermath of the contest that Providence had brought him the victory. Matt Quay, reflecting on these solemn words, rolled his eyes heavenward and chuckled: "Think of the man! He will never know how close many men were compelled to approach the gates of the penitentiary to make him President."

Before he left office, Cleveland had felt reverberations of international politics that gave a forewarning of the struggle over imperialism soon to shake the country. One episode concerned the Samoan archipelago in the South Pacific. After the completion of the transcontinental railroad in 1869, United States trade with Australia and New Zealand had increased markedly. Furthermore, the growing American navy required coaling stations in strategic places. The magnificent harbor of Pago Pago in Samoa seemed made to order for the purpose. By a treaty in 1878, the United States had not only obtained coaling rights in Samoa, but also was committed to acting as mediator in case Samoa and a foreign power became entangled in a dispute.

Britain and Germany also acquired commercial rights in Samoa, and soon the scramble was on to control the islands, with the United States maintaining that Samoa must remain autonomous. In December 1888, the Germans declared war on the puppet Samoan king, and in a humiliating encounter, a party of German sailors was ambushed and killed by Samoans as they came ashore. In this tense moment, there gathered in the islands a fleet consisting of one British, three American, and three German warships, with the British and Americans determined to rein in the Germans. Cleveland thus had a first taste of the imperialistic maneuvering of the great European powers. It did not please him. He would continue to believe that the problems for the nation were homegrown and festering. Early in the Harrison administration, the forces of calm prevailed, and Samoa was placed under a protectorate administered by the three contesting naval powers

Although a lame duck, and taking advantage of that fact, Cleveland, in his fourth annual message, which he sent to Congress on December 8, 1888, spoke robust words of reflection on the first century of the nation's history under the Constitution. He said he gazed upon clear dangers to America's future "happiness and perpetuity." Beneath "the pride and satisfaction" that people must feel about the achievements of a hundred years, "a closer scrutiny develops a somber shading." "We discover," he lamented, "that the fortunes realized by our manufacturers are no longer solely the reward of sturdy industry and enlightened forethought, but that they result from the discriminating favor of the Government and are largely built upon undue exactions from the masses of the people." He went on: "The gulf between employers and the employed is constantly widening, and classes are rapidly forming, one comprising the very rich and powerful, while in another are the toiling poor. . . . We discover the existence of trusts, combinations, and monopolies, while the citizen is struggling far in the rear or is trampled to death beneath an iron heel." He continued relentlessly: "Communism is a hateful thing and a menace to peace and organized government; but the communism of combined wealth and capital, the outgrowth of overweening cupidity and selfishness, which insidiously undermines the justice and integrity of free institutions, is not less dangerous than the communism of oppressed poverty and toil, which, exasperated by injustice and discontent, attacks with wild disorder the citadel of rule."

These carefully hewn expressions of anguish foreshadowed the antitrust fervor that commanded public attention in the progressive era at the beginning of the twentieth century. Cleveland was aware that government intervention was indispensable to the task of arranging social justice. But he was imbued indelibly with the antistatist Jeffersonianism he shared with fellow Bourbons; it prevented him from making legislative proposals to confront what he recognized so clearly. And in a time when a president's annual message was not delivered in person before Congress, the stern phrases that this president proffered had no impact on public policy. The message disappeared into the oblivion of the *Congressional Record*.

Cleveland's work was done. When the outgoing presidential couple prepared to leave the White House, Frances Cleveland was cheerful. As the household staff gathered in the reception hall to bid them Godspeed, she declared to a favorite servant: "I want you to take good care of all the furniture and ornaments in the house, for I want to find everything just as it is now when we come back again." She added, "We are coming back, just four years from today."

Harrison's inauguration took place in a rainstorm of diluvial proportions, although, at his insistence, the new president and Cleveland rode to the Capitol in an open carriage. In a noteworthy show of amity, Cleveland held an umbrella over Harrison's head as he delivered his address. The oath of office was administered by Melville W. Fuller, Cleveland's friend, whom he had recently appointed chief justice. The ensuing parade dragged on into the early evening as the rain continued to fall, but the Republicans gloried in their return to power.

The ball that night, again held at the Pension Building, attracted twelve thousand people celebrating the advent of the centennial president. Harrison disapproved of dancing and alcohol, so the festivities were enlivened only by the Marine Band playing some marches. Out of the spotlight at last, the Clevelands, as a couple, were private citizens for the first time.

7

An Interregnum

Having cleaned out the White House attic, which had over-flowed with the thousands of gifts from admirers in every cor-ner of the country, Grover and Frances Cleveland decided to give up Washington. They sold Oak View and headed for New York. The first stop was the Victoria Hotel, where Cleveland had reserved rooms so that he might take off on a fishing trip to the Adirondacks. Then, after some days during which he was besieged by real estate agents making seductive offers, he finally rented a brownstone house at 816 Madison Avenue, close to Sixty-eighth Street. In 1892, the family moved to a house on West Fifty-first Street, just off Fifth Avenue. Cleveland had cho-sen it because it was next door to the residence of his friend Elias C. Benedict, the wealthy gas magnate.

The Clevelands lived quietly and entertained sparingly, social-izing with only a small circle of intimates. The ex-president enjoyed playing cribbage, and he and Frances Cleveland loved taking in plays and vaudeville shows that were New York City's signature. Serving the former first couple as houseman, butler, and valet was their reliable William Sinclair.

Cleveland was not a rich man, and his presidency had not added to his estate. In Washington he had probably saved around $25,000 a year, about half of his presidential salary. But his psychological need to work, rather than the desire for money, brought him back into the private practice of law. Even before he had settled into ex-presidential life, he was much sought after as a "name partner" by members of the New York bar. The doyen of the legal fraternity, Joseph H. Choate, upon Cleveland's arrival in the city, had immediately arranged a dinner in his honor. But Cleveland, through his friendship with Francis Stetson, a member of Bangs, Stetson, Tracy, and MacVeagh, decided to associate himself with that firm as "of counsel" to it. He did not share in the firm's income, but he contributed his portion to the rental of the group of suites it occupied. Nor did he, as a rule, participate in the firm's practice. He relied mainly on the courts to send him referee work to which he applied himself with his customary diligence.

Stetson, a good conversationalist and a splendid lawyer, took over J. P. Morgan's account after the death of Albert Tracy, Stetson's partner, who was Morgan's brother-in-law. Through this connection, Cleveland came to know Morgan well; they often could be seen in lively conversation both in the law office and at the Downtown Association, where Cleveland frequently took lunch, or at the Century Club, of which he and Morgan were members, situated at Fifteenth Street until its removal to Forty-third Street, its present location, in 1891.

Through their friend Richard Watson Gilder, editor of the *Century* magazine (unrelated to the club), the Clevelands were introduced to the calm and special beauty of Cape Cod, together with the excellent fishing in Buzzards Bay. After scouting, they decided to purchase a cottage on Monument Point in 1891. Of all the dwellings that the Clevelands occupied in their still recent marriage, this two-story clapboard house, which they called Gray Gables, was their favorite. There they could relax quite near and yet far enough from the world of affairs that claimed the other part of their lives.

While their address in New York was still Madison Avenue, Frances Cleveland gave birth to Ruth, the first of their five children. Cleveland, now fifty-four years old, who had always enjoyed the company of children, was filled with ineffable joy. He wrote Bissell, also about to become a father for the first time, that he felt as if "he had entered the real world" at last. Other children followed in rapid succession: Esther in 1893, Marion in 1895, Richard Folsom in 1897, Francis Grover in 1903. Ruth was destined not to reach the age of thirteen, dying of diphtheria in 1904. She lives in the national memory as Baby Ruth, the name that newspapers bestowed on her and that in 1921 the Curtiss Company decided to assign to a candy bar, still popular today.

Cleveland never took his eyes off the administration that had ousted him from office. Today, it is hard to know whether he privately sought vindication from the people, or whether he was bored by his life in retirement, or whether he was genuinely eager to finish the work that had been interrupted by the election of 1888.

There was much in the Harrison presidency that distressed Cleveland. He saw his old rival, Blaine, who had helped get Harrison the nomination in 1888, once more named secretary of state. John Wanamaker, a wealthy Philadelphia merchant, had become postmaster general. Indeed, there were so many heads of companies in the cabinet that it was tagged "The Businessman's Cabinet." Moreover, these men had followed traditional practice: Wanamaker, for one, fired some thirty thousand Democrats in his department to make room for Republicans. Under the guidance of House Speaker Thomas B. Reed, "pork-barrel bills" of all kinds were passed, to the delight of greedy interests everywhere. Harrison even signed a bill that provided a pension for every Union veteran—making Cleveland feel personally rebuked.

On top of everything, Congress passed the highest tariff in American history; it bore the name of its principal advocate, Representative William McKinley of Ohio. The duty on raw sugar was removed, but American sugar growers were compensated by a bounty of two cents a pound for their crop. The tariff on manufactured goods was set so high—an average of 12 percent higher than it had been—that farmers, traditionally reliable Republicans, were irate, seeing that the manufactured products they needed would be more expensive than ever. This rural wing of the Republican Party was mollified somewhat by the passage of the Sherman Silver Purchase Act, which increased the amount of silver purchased by the federal government each year and allowed the issuance of paper money backed by silver. Finally—John Sherman's other contribution—the Sherman Anti-trust Act had the appearance of eliminating monopolies that acted "in restraint of trade." It was a bipartisan measure designed to placate the public. Business leaders acquiesced in its passage because they regarded it as innocuous. The surplus that Cleveland had worried about so much was no more, and the country was operating in deficit. There were then many matters for the Democrats to clamor about as they set their sights on the next presidential election. Cleveland watched all of this but kept his counsel. He was observing the old rule that ex-presidents do not comment publicly on the work of their successors.

The midterm election of 1890, though, produced alarming results. "Slack-water politics" was ending at last as much of rural America was smoldering in revolt and seeking reform through the ballot box. Farmers in the South and West had been rousing themselves since the 1870s. They had created pressure groups called Farmers' Alliances, whose demands shook the business community. They called for more paper money in circulation, on the theory that there simply was not enough money available for "the money work," by which they meant the ability to buy goods at reasonable prices and make mortgage payments easily.

Eventually there were two major voices representing the farmers: the Southern Alliance and the Northwestern Alliance. The Southern Alliance became, by virtue of its three million white members and its affiliated Colored Farmers' Alliance numbering one million black members, the dominant one. In 1889, an attempt to merge the alliances, along with representatives of labor, thus uniting "the organized tillers and the organized toilers," failed. The Southern Alliance had insisted on separate white and black lodges, which the Northwestern Alliance would not accept.

The slowness with which farmers organized their forces deserves a word of explanation. The telephone had not yet entered their working lives, so communication was slow. More important, the Civil War had created bonds to the established parties that farming people broke only slowly. Most farmers in the Northwest, for example, felt they could not forsake the Republican Party, the party of Lincoln and Grant, who had saved the Union. And to white farmers of the South, the Democratic Party was no less dear as defender of the Lost Cause of the Confederacy.

But hard times beginning in the late 1880s helped weaken these old political loyalties. Falling prices for wheat and cotton as a result of competition from abroad was one element causing distress. Another was terrible weather in 1885 and 1887, devastating to cattlemen and to grain growers. A third factor was the perceived excess in the high rates that railroads charged for shipping to market.

The most punishing circumstance, however, was the mortgage burden borne by almost every farmer. These inescapable obligations had been entered into in order to put up farm buildings and fences and to buy necessary equipment and supplies. The mortgages were usually held by a local bank that had ties to a correspondent bank in the East. Thus the banks and the railroads were the farmers' principal "enemies," and "Wall Street" became the great symbol of oppression. As the editor of a farm journal expressed the situation from the farmers' viewpoint:

> There are three great crops raised in Nebraska. One is a crop of corn, one is a crop of freight rates, and one a crop of interest. One is produced by farmers who by sweat and toil farm the land. The other two are produced by men who sit in their offices and behind their bank counters and farm the farmers.

The currency question had also been bedeviling the political scene for many years. During most of the early history of the United States, gold and silver coins had circulated side by side.

In 1834 the metals had been valued at a ratio of 16 to 1, meaning sixteen ounces of silver were worth one ounce of gold. After gold was discovered in California in 1849, gold became more plentiful, and gradually its value dropped in relation to silver. People soon noticed that the silver in a silver dollar was worth more than the gold in a gold dollar. Hence, very little silver was brought to the United States Mint for coining—so little, in fact, that in 1873 Congress took silver off the list of metals to be coined. Such supply as there was went to silversmiths instead, where umbrella handles, silver ornamented hair brushes, snuff boxes, and other items were fashioned for sale in fine stores.

But beginning in the late 1870s, newly opened silver mines in the Rockies were pouring out their product in ever-increasing amounts. Silversmiths could not absorb it all, even as the price fell lower and lower. The mine operators began to decry the "Crime of '73" and demand that the government purchase silver for coins once more. An act of Congress in 1878 authorized the government to buy between two million and four million dollars' worth of silver each month. The silver men were still not satisfied. The admission to the Union of a number of silver-producing states in 1889 and 1890 increased the pressure on Congress to buy even more silver for the U.S. Mint. The Sherman Silver Purchase Act of 1890 was an answer: it increased the quantity of silver the government could take in for minting and allowed it to issue paper money backed by silver.

These economic developments brought the farmers and the silver men together. Silver people, seeking to strengthen their base of support, affirmed that the farmers' desperate call for cheaper money could be met by the unlimited coinage of silver. The farmers, for their part, were pleased to have the affluent mine owners as allies and fellow agitators.

Farmers, however, were interested in more than the currency. Meeting in 1889 in St. Louis, representatives of the alliances adopted a wide-ranging political platform that called for a graduated income tax, government ownership of the railroads, and an end to national banks. Joining with Democrats in many places, the Southern Alliance in 1890 captured four governorships, forty-six seats in the House of Representatives, three seats in the Senate, and control of eight state legislatures. On the Plains, the Northwestern Alliance sent six representatives to Congress from Kansas and Nebraska.

As Cleveland watched the rise of discontent, he continued his principled silence about it. He spent much of his time at Gray Gables. Then, slowly, he began to have his say, not criticizing the Harrison administration directly, but mostly restating his old positions. In March 1890, for instance, he traveled to Steubenville, Ohio, to tell the local Lodge of the Farmers' Alliance of the baleful effects of the tariff on their well-being. No group seemed too unimportant to spend time with. He even stood before the annual banquet of the Piano and Organ Manufacturers, to praise American industry and assure his audience that "happy is the son or daughter who can place among his or her household goods the old piano."

In a letter of February 10, 1891, to the chairman of the Reform Club meeting in New York that was called to voice opposition to the free coinage of silver, Cleveland broke with the congressional Democrats. Agreeing heartily with the purport of the gathering, he put himself on record as firmly against such a "dangerous and reckless experiment." He obviously had in mind becoming president again. As the year went on, he was making a public address at the rate of almost once a month. That was a busy schedule for one who did not enjoy platform speaking. He told the German Young Men's Association of the value of the German population to America. He warned the Commercial Club of Providence, Rhode Island, against "the evil tendencies of private and special legislation, whatever its guise." On October 27, 1891, in Madison Square Garden, speaking to the Business Men's Democratic Association, he reaffirmed his belief that "if a few businessmen could be substituted for professional men in official places, the people would positively gain by the exchange." December found him trying his hand at humor when he apologized to the New England Society for having been born in New Jersey, and boasting that his father had been a native of Connecticut.

He also took note of the seething disaffection brewing in the land. Speaking in Tremont Temple in Boston on October 31, he reiterated an old theme of his: "A condition of restlessness and irritation has grown up throughout the country, born of prevailing inequality and unfairness, which threatens an attack upon sound currency, and which awakens the fear and anxious solicitude of thoughtful and patriotic men." Patently, as 1892 approached, Cleveland was ready to run again, his natural conservatism having likely been reinforced by his associations at the law firm. No doubt too he was encouraged by his young wife, eager to redeem her promise to return to Washington as first lady. Nevertheless, he was determined not to fight for the nomination; his friends would have to deliver it to him.

The Democratic convention assembled in a specially constructed building in Chicago on June 21, 1892. Optimistic that Cleveland had retired from active politics, David B. Hill, Cleveland's successor as governor and now senator, eagerly sought the nomination. He could see that Cleveland's stand on the money question had alienated many western and southern Democrats. And Tammany Hall, Hill reckoned, would not support Cleveland; indeed, it demonstrated vigorously against its old foe on the convention floor. Bourke Cockran, one of the wigwam's veteran chieftains, scalded the former president in a stem-winder delivered at two o'clock in the morning.

In spite of all this, on the first ballot Cleveland received the required two-thirds majority of the delegates' votes. Hill's highhanded seizure of control of the New York delegation had offended too many in the convention to bring him the support he hoped he would have. Crestfallen, he went off in a sulk and took solace in the thought that to carry New York, Cleveland would have to beg for his support. Nominated for vice president was Adlai E. Stevenson of Illinois, a free-silver advocate. A former member of the House, he had been assistant postmaster general under Cleveland. In that post Stevenson had fired forty thousand Republican officeholders to make room for Democrats. His opponents castigated him as the Headsman. On the all-important money question, the Democratic platform straddled. It made a strong declaration that "the federal government has no constitutional power to impose and collect tariff duties, except for purposes of revenue only."

In the Republican camp there was little enthusiasm for the president in office. A dump-Harrison movement was led by Tom Platt and other discontented party leaders. They included Thomas B. Reed, Speaker of the House, and Matt Quay, senator from Pennsylvania, who, as chairman of the Republican National Committee, as we saw, had helped bring victory for Harrison four years earlier. These men felt sure that Harrison, unbending and aloof and almost unapproachable, was a loser. In addition to disliking him personally, party spokesmen were still smarting from the independence he had shown in doling out jobs. Yet, the keenly sensitive historian Henry Adams would later write that Harrison was the best president the country had had since Lincoln.

The party bigwigs hoped to again run Blaine, the secretary of state, even though he had not declared himself a candidate. Blaine had remained a giant of the party, and in his capacity as the senior cabinet officer, under the Presidential Succession Act that Cleveland had signed in 1886, he was next in line to the president and vice president. In the end, the party had no choice but to renominate Harrison, relying on the hope that people respected him as a family man devoted to the cause of temperance. For vice president, the convention chose Whitelaw Reid, publisher of the *New York Tribune*.

Meanwhile, given their stunning successes at the polls in 1890, the farm leadership was ready to carry their crusade to victory. This election of 1892 was the longed-for opportunity. Meeting in Omaha, with much fanfare, the farm spokesmen brought forward the People's Party, quickly known as the Populist Party. It reached out to all the aggrieved. The extensive platform added to the farmers' old list of demands a fervent plea for the free and unlimited coinage of silver in the ratio of 16 to 1; generous pensions for Union veterans; the direct election of senators; the adoption of the secret ballot in elections; the establishment of the eight-hour day for working people; and a one-term limit for the president and vice president.

With the fervor of a religious revival, the Populists went on to nominate for president James B. Weaver of Iowa, whose valorous leadership as a Union officer had won him the brevet of brigadier general. He then served a term in Congress as a "soft-money" man—a Greenbacker. Now as an ardent supporter of the Farmers' Alliance and a superb orator, he appeared the ideal choice. The vice presidential candidate was James G. Field of Virginia, a former Confederate general who had been runner-up in the balloting for standard-bearer. Notably, only a small minority of the Southern Alliance backed the People's Party, largely because it had the potential to weaken white supremacy.

Helping beat the drums for Weaver and the radical cause he represented were a colorful lot who rallied the troops and garnered nationwide publicity. One of them was "Pitchfork Ben" Tillman, who became governor of South Carolina in 1890. When he ran for the Senate in 1894, he shouted memorably to his frenzied followers, "Send me to Washington and I'll stick a pitchfork into [Cleveland's] old ribs." Tom Watson of Georgia was another resolute spokesman for downtrodden farmers; he sought to advance their interests in the House of Representatives. Kansas provided at least three leaders who earned popular attention: Annie Diggs, a talented editor and fiery organizer; Mary Ellen Lease, known as a "Patrick Henry in petticoats," who advised farmers to "raise less corn and more hell"; and "Sockless" Jerry Simpson, who had been elected to the House of Representatives in 1890. He earned his nickname after he ridiculed a political rival—a banker—for wearing silk socks. A newspaper reporter deduced from the charge that Simpson wore none.

Cleveland and Harrison might as well have lived on a different planet from these men and women. Still they were mindful of—possibly intimidated by—the verbal ferocity of the farm radicals. It assuredly enlisted the attention of newspaper editors and their readers. People everywhere expected the consequence of the passionate Populist campaigning would be to split the Democratic Party in the South and split the Republican Party in the Midwest. Plainly the old party ties would dissolve and new ones would be formed.

The actual canvass did nothing of the sort. It was the dullest in memory. It turned out fewer brass bands and generated fewer torchlight parades and rallies than anybody could remember. William McKinley of Ohio campaigned vigorously for Harrison, but Harrison gave up his own efforts when the first lady, Caroline Scott Harrison, died suddenly in late October. Out of respect, the ever-punctilious Cleveland stopped campaigning also.

In New York, acting as a go-between, Cleveland's former cabinet officer, the energetic William C. Whitney, arranged a dinner at the Victoria Hotel for Tammany honchos and Cleveland in order to help bury the hatchet. It is not clear what took place that night. It is said that the chiefs virtually demanded of Cleveland that in the event of his election, he give Hill and his confreres control of the federal patronage in New York. Cleveland, of course, would give no such commitment, and everyone at the table must have known that it was improper to ask for a promise of that kind. At any rate, the party regulars had no choice. It was time to make up and shake hands. All present knew that the party could not afford to alienate the reformers who had always been the backbone of Cleveland's success at the polls. The dinner ended on a friendly note. Not until near the end of September, though, did Hill publicly speak on behalf of the party ticket. It helped guarantee that this time New York would be in the Democratic column in November.

The parties were competing in a grim atmosphere. A strike in the spring of 1892 at the Carnegie Steel Corporation in Homestead, Pennsylvania, demonstrated this fact and shook the nation as yet another omen of what might lie ahead. Workers at the plant had refused to accept proposed wage cuts and had gone on strike. Thereupon Henry Clay Frick, Andrew Carnegie's right-hand man, shut down the plant entirely and surrounded it with guards. The enraged strikers beat up the guards and ran them out of town, fearing they had been brought in in order to reopen the plant with strikebreakers. The company responded: it hired three hundred Pinkerton "detectives" and towed them up the Monongahela River toward Homestead. The strikers, behind barricades, opened fire as the detectives came ashore. What ensued was a pitched battle, and when it ended thirteen hours later with the surrender of the detectives, ten men lay dead and dozens wounded. The Carnegie Corporation then persuaded the governor of Pennsylvania to send in the militia to restore peace. The men who struck were not rehired, and the nascent union was broken.

Some members of Congress sympathized with the strikers, but most Americans still believed that working people ought to be able to sell their services as individuals and as they saw fit. Nevertheless, while the public was critical of the violence of the strikers, it could see that the steel interests were benefiting from the high McKinley tariff and refusing to share some of the benefits. On balance, the Republican cause was hurt by the strike. In accepting his third nomination by the party, Cleveland spoke feelingly, denouncing in uncommonly fresh phrases the crushing of the steel workers' union as "the tender mercy the working-man receives from those made selfish and sordid by unjust governmental favoritism."

The verdict on November 8 was that Cleveland would have a second term. With about twelve million citizens going to the polls, he had defeated Harrison in popular votes by more than a third of a million. In the electoral college he overwhelmed his opponent 277 to 145. Harrison had lost even his home state of Indiana. The Populist Weaver, in an amazing performance, captured a million popular votes and 22 votes in the electoral college. Cleveland's victory, though, was broad. In addition to the solid Democratic South, with the heavy support of conservative business and financial groups, he had won in the East and in California and in the industrial states everywhere. His unwavering backing of the gold standard against the silver forces had carried the day. Into the bargain, for the first time since 1858, the Democrats had won not only the White House but also control of both houses of Congress.

8

The Return to Power

On March 2 the Clevelands, who were living in a cottage in Lakewood, New Jersey, put at their disposal by Nathan Strauss, the philanthropist and co-owner of R. H. Macy & Co., departed for Washington and Cleveland's second inauguration. The bright sunshine that people called Cleveland Luck seemed the augury of a good presidential term ahead. The president-elect and his party took rooms in the District at the Arlington Hotel. On the following morning, Cleveland went to the White House to pay a courtesy call on Harrison, and Harrison reciprocated the call that afternoon. In the evening, Cleveland and his wife dined at the White House with Harrison and his daughter Mary—just the four of them. Then, as they ate, the Cleveland Luck ran out: it began to rain, and the rain soon turned to snow. By morning a full-scale blizzard was closing down the city.

On Saturday, Cleveland went over to Willard's Hotel for breakfast, a gustatory experience he had long enjoyed. Nathaniel Hawthorne once wrote that the Willard, located only two blocks from the White House, "may be more justly called the center of Washington and the Union than either the Capitol, the White House or the State Department." An important reason was the renowned breakfast menu. Available until eleven every morning, it included such treats as fried oysters, pâté de fois gras, steak and onions, blanc mange, and game birds served on toast. Cleveland may have known that Lincoln's first meal in the District when he arrived in 1861 for *his* inauguration was breakfast at the Willard.

On this day there, Cleveland was the honored guest of one hundred New York businessmen who had journeyed to the city on the overnight train to be his escort at the festivities. It was not lost on anyone that this spectacle would be a fitting symbol for the new administration.

The falling temperature and the driving wind had frozen the snow tight on the roads. But the storm was abating, and the streets were slippery and slushy; Pennsylvania Avenue seemed deserted. The bleachers prepared for a jubilant throng were empty and covered with snow; in some places they collapsed under its weight. When Cleveland and Harrison headed for the Capitol from the White House, only the military—including a unit of Marines—and the businessmen slogged along to accompany them.

As spectators and participants alike shivered in the wind at the plaza in front of the Capitol's East Portico, the president-elect finally appeared on the platform about one o'clock, his mustache flecked with tiny crystals of ice. Wasting no time, he stepped forward resolutely and took off his hat, ignoring shouts that he keep it on in the cold. Holding it at his left side, he delivered the inaugural address—from memory like the first, although this one was slightly longer. He dwelt on familiar themes and goals: a bridling of monopolies—which are "inconsistent with the fair field that ought to be open to every independent activity"; the crying need for better treatment of the Indians—who must be "defended against the cupidity of designing men"; and a lowered tariff—resulting in "a more just and equitable system of Federal taxation." All this, he said, must be accomplished "without heedless vindictiveness," for, he added, "our mission is not punishment, but the rectification of wrong."

At its conclusion, Chief Justice Fuller administered the oath of office. Once again Cleveland had reversed the usual order of procedure and opted to be sworn in after his address. As the crowd broke up, the Clevelands rode to the White House for lunch. In the middle of the afternoon, soon fairly trembling in the cold, they sat in the reviewing stand to watch a parade that lasted three hours, intent on seeing it to the end. That night the Pension Building was once more the scene of the inaugural ball.

The first family did not immediately take up residence at the White House. They lived for a time at the Admiral Porter House on H Street, promptly labeled "The Little White House." Out of concern for their infant, Ruth, not yet a year and a half old, they had held off moving into their familiar old quarters, fearing scarlet fever, which had recently infected a Harrison grandchild. When they finally established themselves in the executive mansion again, they would find it now had some rooms lighted by electricity for the first time. The Clevelands had already had experience with electric illumination in New York, unlike the Harrisons who, fearing they would be electrocuted by touching the switch, left the lights burning all night and relied on an engineer to arrive in the morning to turn them off.

Despite the brief delay in taking over the White House, the work of shaping the administration went on without pause. The cabinet, in potential, was as outstanding as the first. Cleveland had said he would not name again those who had served in his first administration. This time Bissell was a member, chosen to be postmaster general, and Lamont became secretary of war. An unprecedented appointment brought to the Department of State Walter Q. Gresham of Illinois, recently a Republican, who in 1888 had been the second choice behind Harrison for the party's nomination but had gone over to the Democrats and had voted for Cleveland. The brilliant Richard B. Olney of Massachusetts came in as attorney general. Little known outside his home state, he was a man of forbidding mien and manner and, in time, only slightly softened by the social world of Washington. When Gresham died in 1895, Olney became secretary of state. In both cabinet offices he left marks on the administration's accomplishments second only to the president's in importance and implication.

As Cleveland's new term opened, hard times—the depression of 1893—struck the country. Thousands of businesses failed, farm prices fell, and it was estimated that a fifth of all factory workers lost their jobs. Some Democrats blamed the Republicans, indicting especially the McKinley tariff, pointing out that it had rendered imports too expensive and produced a decline in customs revenue.

Cleveland believed that prosperity could be restored only if Americans once more had confidence in the backing of their paper money. He felt sure that their faith in the nation's currency had been shaken by the Sherman Silver Purchase Act. He maintained that basing the currency on both gold and silver as that law provided was draining away the nation's gold supply. Because silver had been made so abundant, it was cheap. As a result, people were using silver to obtain paper money, converting the papers into gold—and then hoarding it. Banks as well as individuals engaged in this practice, and in so doing were threatening the nation's gold reserves. The only solution, Cleveland believed, was to place the country on a gold standard; that is, having a currency based solely on gold. Pursuing this conviction, he persuaded Congress to repeal the Silver Purchase Act before the first year of his term was over.

In the presence of declining revenue, the Treasury faced the need, with reduced means, to pay government expenses. Secretary Carlisle proposed to float a bond issue for sale to the public in order to restock the reserve. The proposal met with little response. The situation grew so critical in 1894 that, early in the next year, Cleveland sent for his friend and former luncheon companion J. P. Morgan; he persuaded Morgan and a banking syndicate that Morgan formed to purchase with gold sixty million dollars in U.S. bonds, favorably priced for the bankers. The "gold deal," as the public came to call it, would yield 3.5 million ounces of gold for the Treasury—one half of it to come from abroad.

The bold step caused a furor. The president, screamed his critics, was in league with the "money trust," once more skinning the ordinary folk. The terms that the syndicate exacted were rightly regarded as exorbitant, and Cleveland's reputation was not enhanced when Morgan refused to tell a congressional committee what his profit had come to. The condemnation of Cleveland is probably unfair because Cleveland bargained hard and, in the acute crisis, had no other way out. To allow the government to go on a silver standard would have shaken the business community and the confidence in America in international banking circles. Cleveland could take credit for having stabilized the currency and stemmed the outflow of gold—although the drain persisted for a number of years. In the eyes of many people, Cleveland, once called Grover the Good, would ever afterward be regarded as a feckless tool of Wall Street bankers.

Only two months after his inauguration, Cleveland had begun to require medical help. He had developed a lesion in his mouth that was quickly diagnosed as a cancer, requiring immediate attention. Possibly, although there is no record that anyone said so at the time, the tumor had been caused by his use of chewing tobacco. The stakes were high, not only for the president but for the nation. The monied interests were relying implicitly on Cleveland to protect them from the nefarious designs of the "silver monomaniacs." If this ardent champion of their position should die, Adlai E. Stevenson, the vice president, a darling of the silver forces who had been made the president's running mate solely for that reason, would sit in the White House. The alarm bells rang loudly, for the stock market could fall and the economy sink to the bottom.

The urgent surgery on the president, therefore, was planned to be carried out in utter secrecy. Cleveland's famous dictum, "Tell the truth," went by the boards. It must be said, though, that the health of presidents was only beginning to be of public interest and concern, and the idea that the chief executive must reveal intimate facts about his personal well-being had not yet emerged. In Victorian America, as in Victorian England, even prying journalists knew that intimate matters concerning the body—and especially that of a respected public figure—were off limits. Chester Arthur, a decade earlier, had kept quiet the fact that he suffered from Bright's disease, a serious ailment. While Woodrow Wilson's massive stroke in 1919 was world-wide news, Franklin D. Roosevelt's heart ailment and John F. Kennedy's Addison's disease were not made known until after their deaths. Openness about the president's medical history has come only gradually.

Some of the details of Cleveland's treatment today have the aspect of bad theater. Because taking Cleveland to a clinic or hospital created a high risk of letting the cat out of the bag, the work was to be done on New York's East River aboard the yacht of a friend, "Commodore" Benedict. Anchored near Bellevue Hospital, the medical staff was ordered to stay indoors lest they be recognized by Bellevue resident doctors. To keep the president steady during the procedure as the boat edged its way northward, his chair was lashed tight to the mast. The principal surgeon was Dr. James D. Bryant, assisted by Dr. William W. Keen, a Philadelphia man who had served in the Civil War and had studied abroad. Indeed, to avoid doing external surgery on Cleveland's face and jaw, Keen used a cheek retractor that he had brought from Paris in 1866. Operated on again a few weeks later, Cleveland was then fitted with an artificial jaw. The prosthesis left his appearance and speech unaffected. And after a stay at Gray Gables, somewhat thinner and somewhat more irascible, the president was back at his desk, slaving away as usual. In spite of rumors at the time, the general public was none the wiser until 1917 when Dr. Keen, in an article in the *Saturday Evening Post*, at last broke the embargo on the story.

The years 1894–95 were not a happy time for the administration. Cleveland had continued to hammer away on the need for a lower tariff. He did not succeed. In 1894, the House of Representatives passed the Wilson-Gorman bill, which provided for considerably lower rates, but in the Senate so many amendments were added that the final product was almost as protectionist as the McKinley tariff. Cleveland inveighed against the bill but allowed it to become law without his signature. The act also provided for an income tax, which had been one of the Populist demands. The Supreme Court, by a narrow margin the following year, declared this provision unconstitutional. The decision added to the hostility felt by farm and labor masses toward Washington.

No politicians, from the president on down, were prepared to directly help the victims of the economic slump. That kind of caring government was still in the distant future. What is more, in the years of the interregnum, Cleveland had become much more sympathetic to the needs and concerns of businessmen and eastern bankers. Nor was he alone in his inclination. Quite simply, the leaders of both parties were impervious to the cries of farmers and workingmen.

People everywhere were appalled when the disaffected began to demonstrate in protest. While the Wilson-Gorman bill was before Congress, a number of ragtag "armies" of farmers and unemployed workers were preparing to march on Washington to demand help in their plight. One of these that gained national attention was under the leadership of "General" Jacob S. Coxey of Massillon, Ohio. Coxey was a wealthy businessman with a plan. He proposed that Congress enact a good roads bill that would put the jobless to work, while adding to the currency three hundred million dollars in bills stated to be legal tender for all transactions.

Accompanied by about a hundred marchers and his infant son—aptly named Legal Tender Coxey—he and his "army" picked up followers on the way, including many newspaper correspondents. Traveling about fifteen miles a day and sleeping under tents, they relied on handouts from sympathetic local people, many of them union members. But the bedraggled ranks slowly disintegrated and reached Washington on May 1, 1894, numbering no more than four hundred forlorn souls. The hard journey ended in grim disappointment: Coxey was arrested for walking on the grass at the Capitol and spent twenty days in jail.

Despite this debacle, the country was alarmed, some people imagining that a bloody revolution was about to erupt. Their fears were heightened when a strike broke out in the same month against the Pullman Company, halting all railroad trains that carried Pullman cars. The walkout had been brewing for some time because anger was fierce against George Pullman, the man whose sleeping car had revolutionized overnight rail travel. He had built a model company town near Chicago, in which his employees were obliged to live. The pretty village with its trim houses and green landscaping was, in fact, an instrument of corporate despotism, reproved even by other leaders of big business.

The rents Pullman charged were excessive, running about 25 percent higher than in neighboring towns. He sold at ten cents per thousand gallons water that he bought from Chicago at four cents. He forced his tenants to buy their food and other necessities from company stores, where prices far exceeded those of regular outlets. The simmering cauldron of protest boiled over when in 1894 the company cut wages an average of 25 percent, without a comparable cut in rent or in the cost of necessities. Pullman refused to listen to complaints and dismissed from their jobs those who persisted in the outcry. He then closed the plant.

At this juncture, the American Railway Union, which had a membership of 150,000, including several thousand Pullman employees, joined the struggle, ordering its members not to handle trains with Pullman cars attached. The strike was quickly turned into a national disruption. Within a month, railroad traffic, particularly in the western states, was almost at a standstill. The beset railroad owners hit on the scheme of coupling Pullman cars to trains that carried mail, confident that any interference with the mail was a federal crime. When the strikers still refused to man the trains, the railroads persuaded Attorney General

Olney to swear in an army of special deputies—actually in the pay of the railroads—in order to help keep the trains moving.

The leader of the union was Eugene V. Debs, a gentle but dynamic person who had made the interests of workingmen the consuming enthusiasm of his life. He had instructed his members to avoid violence. But it broke out now anyhow between the deputies and the strikers. The railroads in their frustration asked President Cleveland to send federal troops to keep order and to guarantee the safe handling of the mails.

Cleveland himself hoped to avoid federal intervention. But Olney put heavy pressure on him. Olney, hot-tempered and wrathful, was openly sympathetic to the railroads, having served railroads as a lawyer in private life. The focus of the struggle was the city of Chicago, the railroad hub of the country. There public opinion was being aroused against the strikers. Scare headlines in the *Chicago Tribune* such as "Mobs Bent on Ruin" and "Debs Is a Dictator" kept the heat high. Hysterical sentiments fed on the fact that one hundred thousand homeless and unemployed people were on the city streets, many of them having drifted in from all parts of the country the year before, seeking work at the Columbian Exposition—which Cleveland had opened officially in May of the previous year. During the exceptionally cold winter that followed, the city fathers had allowed many of these unfortunates to find shelter in City Hall.

Olney insisted that troops were needed to restore order and move the mail. Despite the argument of Governor John P. Altgeld of Illinois that they were not necessary, that local authorities were adequate for the purpose, Cleveland yielded and dispatched the soldiers. He chided the governor: "It seems to me that in this hour of danger and public distress, discussion may well give way to active efforts on the part of all in authority to restore obedience to law and to protect life and property." He is supposed also to have said: "If it takes every dollar in the Treasury and every soldier in the United States to deliver a postal card in Chicago, that postal card should be delivered."

When the strike continued, the railroads, under Olney's guidance, obtained an injunction against the union, calling upon it to cease interference with railroad transportation. The strikers violated the injunction, at which point the government moved. Debs was arrested and sent to jail. The strike was broken. Some forty years had to elapse before the use of the injunction to break a strike would be outlawed.

The halfhearted efforts of Attorney General Olney to enforce the Sherman Anti-trust Act produced further despair among many who hoped for a friendlier federal government. His weak presentation of the case against the Sugar Trust, which the Supreme Court dismissed in 1895, was seen widely as evidence that the administration was not interested in social justice. Cleveland never fully agreed with Olney's relaxed attitude toward the trusts, but, being inclined to give his cabinet officers free rein, he supported and even defended Olney against the charge that he was derelict in his duty to uphold the law.

These various displays of the administration at work made men and women all around the country reflect on what the future held for the fate of the republic. Thoughtful people recalled that only a few years earlier—in 1886—Cleveland had dedicated in New York harbor France's glorious gift to the United States, the Statue of Liberty. With trepidation, they brought to mind the noble words inscribed on its base: "I lift my lamp beside the golden door." Would America continue to be a "land of opportunity" for all?

Meanwhile, the nation was looking abroad. The growth of the navy that Cleveland had fostered in his first administration now required coaling facilities in distant places if the vessels were to have range in their operations. In 1887 the United States acquired from the Hawaiian monarchy the right to establish a coaling and repair station at Pearl Harbor, the majestic landlocked bay on the south coast of the island of Oahu. American sugar planters, missionaries, and traders already ensconced in Hawaii were glad to think that the islands might soon come under American protection. The planters had become prosperous after the United States had entered into a treaty with Hawaii in 1875 permitting Hawaiian sugar to enter the United States market without paying a duty.

Several unexpected events provided an opportunity for the settlers, notably the planters, to act. First was the passage of the McKinley tariff, which permitted all foreign sugar—not only that from Hawaii—to enter the United States duty-free. In addition to this competition for their main product, the planters would be further handicapped by the bounty that was to be paid to American producers. In a word, the Americans in Hawaii desired to live under the Stars and Stripes. The second development was the accession of Liliuokalani to the throne of Hawaii in 1891. Unlike her pliant brother, who had just died, Queen "Lil," as she became known in the American press, was a strong-willed woman, understandably suspicious of the loyalty of Americans living in her realm.

The queen's misgivings were confirmed when early in 1893, fearing that Liliuokalani would soon rid her government of American influence, the planters made their move. They organized a revolt, dethroned her, and set up a provisional government. They had been abetted by an American naval force landed on instructions from the U.S. minister in Honolulu. Less than a month of Harrison's administration was left when the president sent to the Senate for ratification a treaty providing for the annexation of Hawaii. The incoming administration had reason to believe that it would be faced with a fait accompli. Public opinion at home seemed to indicate acquiescence. A popular jingle went:

> . . . *Liliuokalani,*
> *Give us your little brown hanni.*

Unmistakably, the sentiment at home was maturing with immense force for the United States to join the great powers of the world in a quest for overseas colonies, sometimes labeled "possessions." To engage in colony building, some advocates believed, could give the nation goals and ideals loftier and more inspiring than the selfish, sordid purposes of businessmen and spoilsmen. The leaders of the movement were often young men who had studied abroad and absorbed the view that the "advanced" nations had a duty to bring "civilization" to the "backward" peoples of color in distant places. Some of the loudest and most articulate voices, identifying themselves with aristocratic Englishmen, accepted the notion of the superiority of white Anglo-Saxon Protestants over all other human types. This idea of racial superiority was reinforced by books on the subject of race and a misreading of Darwin, called Social Darwinism, that seemingly validated a right to govern "inferiors." The rationale also gave these same proponents political leverage over the immigrant masses now crowding into the cities at home.

The map of the world already reflected the spectacular exploits of the Western peoples in their self-appointed mission. The color red usually denoted the British empire, violet the French, and beige the German. For the United States, however, no color was firmly established—in part because its "possessions" were so few, and in part because its career in imperialism had begun so late that the choicest colors were already assigned. In a sentence now famous, Senator Henry Cabot Lodge of Massachusetts would declare: "As one of the great nations of the world, the United States must not fall out of the line of march."

Cleveland, of an older generation than the American Young Turks calling for "possessions," was unimpressed by their arguments. He sided with the coterie of anti-imperialists, who clung to the imperishable ideal of the Declaration that all men have the right to self-government, and that nothing can make this ideal outmoded. Unabashedly, and with a keen sense of justice, upon taking office he withdrew from the Senate Harrison's treaty of annexation. On December 2, 1893, in his annual message, he explained forthrightly that upon investigating the situation in Hawaii, "it seemed to me the only honorable course for our Government to pursue was to undo the wrong that had been done by those representing us and to restore as far as practicable the status at the time of our forcible intervention." Still, the fact was that the queen could be restored to her place only by using force against the Americans who had removed her. Democrats, disappointed in the president's courageous stand, were prone to insist that it was not in the American tradition to put monarchs back on their thrones. Cleveland could do no more, and he turned the question over to Congress. He was gone from the scene when in 1898 Congress approved a resolution annexing Hawaii.

It had come as a relief to many people who felt they were victims of industrial capitalism that Olney moved from the attorney general's office to the Department of State in June 1895. There his opinionated and brusque style might find usefulness. He put it on display in dealing with the long-simmering border dispute between Venezuela and British Guyana that had begun in 1814 when Britain took over that part of the region from the Dutch. The United States had two main interests in this seemingly distant conflict. First, if the British, becoming in the 1890s more aggressive in their demands, were finally to acquire the area in question on the Orinoco River, they would control a vast region on the shoulder of the southern continent. Second, if the recently established Pan-American Union that the United States had fathered was to have meaning, then any perceived violation of the Monroe Doctrine—not to speak of the infringement of a member nation's territory—could not stand.

In Cleveland's first administration an effort at arbitration had been rejected by the British. Harrison too had failed to bring the British to the table. A new chapter in the story began in the fall of 1894 when an incendiary pamphlet, entitled *British Aggression in Venezuela, or the Monroe Doctrine on Trial*, prepared by a lobbyist for Venezuela, was circulated in Washington and proved highly influential, especially with representatives and senators. Early the following year, Congress called upon the president to urge the British and Venezuelan governments to submit their dispute to arbitration. Cleveland was under increasing pressure to show strength, particularly since he had so recently hauled down the flag in Hawaii. He was determined also to succeed in an arbitration effort because he feared that if once the United States was elsewhere engaged, the British would move in on the contended territory and make it their own.

In July 1895, Olney, confirmed as secretary of state only the month before, sent a remarkable note to London. It warned sternly that if Britain were to seize the disputed territory by force, the United States would take action to prevent a violation of the Monroe Doctrine. And the secretary added words that infuriated not only the Britons but Latin Americans as well. "Today," he said in a formulation that lingers in history as the Olney Doctrine, "the United States is practically sovereign on this continent [meaning the Western Hemisphere], and its fiat is law upon the subjects to which it confines its interposition." Further, he declared, the "infinite resources [of the United States] combined with its isolated position render it master of the situation and practically invulnerable as against any and all other powers." This astounding assertion reverberated on both sides of the Atlantic: delight on this side, puzzlement and dismay on the other.

The heavy Irish American constituency of the Democratic Party was all eyes as they watched the president and his people go to the mat with John Bull. Cleveland had his own animus because he could not forget that the blunder of Sackville-West played a part in his losing the election of 1888. Among businesspeople, there was a growing Anglophobia too, based partly on a belief that British trade practices were somehow responsible for the hard times. While not given to grandstanding, the president could see the value of twisting the lion's tail and even tying a knot in it.

Although it is said that Cleveland tried to soften Olney's language somewhat, he went along with the secretary's stern, screaming-eagle message. The British did not flinch. Nor did they respond promptly—to the further irritation of the administration. Finally in November, Lord Salisbury, the foreign secretary, stated in two notes that the Monroe Doctrine did not apply in this case, that the dispute involved "simply the determination of the frontier of a British possession which belonged to the Throne of England long before Venezuela even came into existence. " Americans were not exalted to hear a British interpretation of the meaning of the Monroe Doctrine. Cleveland, incensed, was described by a friend as "mad clear through."

The following month, Cleveland sent Congress a special message he had stayed up all night to write himself, asking for the appointment of a boundary commission and declaring that unless the British accepted arbitration, the United States would use "every means in its power to protect Venezuelan territory." His words were neither conciliatory nor diplomatic, for the message concluded: "There is no calamity which a great nation can invite which equals that which follows a supine submission to wrong and injustice and the consequent loss of national self-respect and honor, beneath which are shielded and defended a people's safety and greatness."

In the ensuing weeks, a call for war was heard throughout the country. Aging Civil War veterans, it was rumored, were ready to answer a summons to duty, and the newspapers were aflame with jingo headlines and editorial shouts for armed action. Irish Americans declared through their organizations that they could field a hundred thousand men. But, as stock prices fell on the rumor of war, and less impetuous people recognized how defenseless were the coastal cities against Britain's naval power, the war fever gradually waned.

The matter dragged on desultorily until it was settled by arbitration in 1899 when Cleveland and Olney were no longer in office. Most people could see that the Venezuela matter was not a vital United States concern. Britain, moreover, was facing greater troubles in South Africa, and it recognized that in a war with the United States it might lose Canada as well as simply the Guyana boundary dispute. Through Olney, and with Cleveland's remarkable compliance, the country had flexed its muscles to the world. The episode had also given the country a "war scare," an experience which that generation had not yet

known. If it frightened people, it also offered a sobering foretaste of what lay only a few years ahead as American isolation
gradually dissolved.

Cleveland did not fail to see that he was battling elements
that were changing the national scene in ways he could not
approve. Addressing a convocation on the occasion of Princeton's sesquicentennial in October 1896, he urged that "educated
men" play a larger role in government and that their work
"would be easier and more useful if it were less spasmodic and
occasional." And in his last annual message, sent to Congress on
December 7, 1896, he was conscious of the effect the civil war
then roiling Cuba was having on the American mind. He knew,
he said, that there were many people who believed the United
States ought to go to war against Spain and settle the matter, and
that the outcome of such a war was certain. "The correctness of
this forecast," he wrote, "need be neither affirmed nor denied."
Nevertheless, he added, "though the Untied States is not a
nation to which peace is a necessity," it has "a character to main-
tain . . . which plainly dictates that right, not might should be
the rule of its conduct." His successor would make the hard
choice.

As that year began, Cleveland could feel the surge of the
younger Democrats bent on establishing new leadership. The
scene was set as 1896 dawned. The Republicans were already
preparing to retake the White House, and they had a candidate:
William McKinley, a Civil War veteran who had twice been
elected governor of Ohio. He was the protégé of Mark Hanna,
an Ohio industrialist, himself the very symbol of the "enemy"
the Populists had in mind. Even before the delegates arrived in
St. Louis in June, McKinley had enough votes to win the nomination on the first ballot. The old warriors, Speaker Reed, Matt
Quay, and Levi P. Morton, were hopefuls, but they received only
token support. Nominated for vice president was Garret A.
Hobart of New Jersey, an ardent drummer for "an honest dollar"
backed by gold.

The platform stated unambiguously that "the existing gold standard must be maintained," although, in a bow to the silverites, it added that it would accept the free coinage of silver if "the leading commercial nations of the world" acquiesced in the establishment of the standard. Some of the silver delegates, dissatisfied with the plank, walked out in protest—a harbinger of what the Democrats might expect when they met shortly. McKinley's own views on the subject were less solid: sometimes he referred to "sound money" and apparently meant he favored the gold standard, and sometimes he seemed to be for bimetalism (money based on both gold and silver). Not for nothing did adversaries call him "Wobbly Willie." But, of course, in carrying water on both shoulders, he hoped to please the traditionally Republican grain growers as well as the traditionally Republican big-business men.

Three weeks later, the Democratic Party assembled in the Coliseum in Chicago to choose a new leader to carry its message. Children approaching adolescence had grown up knowing only Cleveland as the Democrats' voice. Already the party had been weakened by six years of the Populist onslaught. The leaders hoped that free silver, now that the Republicans had passed up the chance, could lead to victory. The silver men, as anticipated, were quickly in control of the proceedings. The platform was readily adopted with the all-important plank calling for the free and unlimited coinage of silver at a ratio of 16 to 1. The huge hall shook to the rafters with a thunderous roar of approval when "Pitchfork Ben" Tillman excoriated Cleveland as "a tool of Wall Street." Such a denunciation at a national convention of a sitting president who was one of the party's own was without precedent. Cleveland never got over the sting.

One of the delegates who had spoken in favor of the platform was William Jennings Bryan, a handsome, strapping, thirty-six-year-old Nebraskan. He had recently been defeated for the Senate after serving two terms in the House of Representatives. A dazzling orator with a melodious voice that carried to the farthest corners of the hall—some people thought it resonated like a pipe organ—he hypnotized the crowd with his delivery. When he reached his final words, the people were on their feet, yelling ecstatically: "You shall not press down upon the brow of labor this crown of thorns, you shall not crucify mankind upon a cross of gold." This and other choice phrases of the speech had been well practiced for years as Bryan traveled about his state championing the cause of silver. He knew what their effect on his hearers would be. So confident indeed was Bryan that he would become the nominee that he had brought his wife with him to witness the event. The speech vaulted him over all the other contenders and on the fifth ballot, as the delegates chanted deliriously "Bryan! Bryan! No crown of thorns, no cross of gold," he became the candidate.

In July when the Populist Party met in St. Louis, they were forlorn and angry: the Democrats had stolen their trump card. One commentator denounced the Democrats as the "cowbird of the reform movement"—a reference to a bird that stashes its eggs in other birds' nests. The Populists had no choice except to support Bryan. But whereas, to balance the ticket, the Democrats had nominated Arthur Sewall of Maine, a banker, to be vice president, the Populists gagged at the thought and named Tom Watson. Watson had said that the Democrats seemed to want the Populists to "play Jonah while they play the whale."

Cleveland watched all of this from Gray Gables with dismay. Many gold Democrats had been advocating a third term for him, and when he failed to stop this boom he may have handicapped the party in finding a substitute candidate. In September, the gold Democrats, creating what was called the National Democratic, or Sound Money, Party, went to Indianapolis for their gathering. Upon being urged to accept their nomination, Cleveland sent one of his insistent backers a definitive response: "My judgment and personal inclination are so unalterably opposed to your suggestion that I cannot for a moment entertain it."

The rump convention turned to John M. Palmer of Illinois for president and to Simon Buckner of Kentucky, a legendary

Confederate general, for vice president. Cleveland and all the members of Cleveland's cabinet, except Hoke Smith, the secretary of the interior, supported Palmer. Smith, a Georgian and owner of the *Atlanta Journal*, felt he had no choice but to support Bryan as the choice of the party of white supremacy. Cleveland understood Smith's position but asked for his resignation anyway, even though the administration had only a few months left in office. Cleveland wrote him a cordial letter of appreciation for his service, and the following year when the cabinet gathered for its annual dinner at the White House, he invited Smith.

If Cleveland felt keenly the party's rejection of him, he said not a word publicly about it throughout the heated campaign. Meanwhile, Bryan waged a fiery crusade for the White House. In so doing, he furthered the modern form of presidential canvass, in which candidates themselves play the chief part. On some days he made as many as six speeches. He tried to persuade the voters that he represented "the people" against "Wall Street." The Republicans campaigned along traditional lines. McKinley, a devoted husband, refused to be away from his ailing wife, so he conducted a "front porch campaign." Thousands of people were brought each week to his house in Canton, Ohio, where he greeted and addressed them. He kept in touch with his party's politicians by telephone, becoming the first nominee to use it extensively in conducting a campaign.

On Election Day, McKinley won convincingly. He carried not only the industrial states but also the important farming states of Iowa, Minnesota, and North Dakota. Farmers had, no doubt, been influenced in his favor by a slight rise in wheat prices at the end of the summer. But many workingmen also went for McKinley, fearing that the inflation Bryan's proposals might lead to would hurt their wages. Cleveland was delighted by the outcome. It seemed to him a vindication of his long support of "sound money." Some journalists even regarded McKinley's triumph as a victory for Cleveland.

9

End of the Road

The Clevelands once more put their minds on leaving Washington and readjusting their lives. Even as the country had its eyes fixed on the election, the bloody insurrection in Cuba was seizing national attention. Cleveland's firm position was to remain neutral. Secretary of State Olney in 1896 sent the Spanish foreign office a note urging the government to make concessions to the *insurrectos*, an impertinent suggestion rejected out of hand. Above all, the administration stood fast against the interventionist claques forming in Congress. Cleveland, though, was once again a lame duck. Cast aside by his party, which had then proceeded to lose the election, Cleveland had lost his political footing.

When McKinley's inauguration approached, the Clevelands, in accordance with recent practice, invited the McKinleys to an informal dinner. The custom was for the men to discuss matters of state and the women to go over details of managing the White House. This time, the ailing Ida McKinley, pleading indisposition, did not accompany her husband. She remained at the Ebbitt House, an apartment hotel in downtown Washington, where McKinley, being a member of the House of Representatives, had long occupied a suite. When he arrived for the dinner, he found his host severely hobbled, his foot heavily bandaged as

a result of a severe attack of gout. There was no awkward-
ness between them: more than once in the previous four years,
McKinley had come over to the White House to visit with Cleveland, whom he greatly admired. The president reciprocated the
warm regard. Moreover, the results of the election, vindicating
in its way Cleveland's support of sound money, sealed a solid
bond between the men. As the evening wore on, they pondered
international affairs together, McKinley expressing the hope
that peace with Spain would continue to hold. Later, Cleveland
would recall the sober grimness of their conversation.

On March 4, when McKinley arrived at the White House to
pick up Cleveland for the ride to the Capitol, the president was
still meeting with his cabinet on official business. When at last
he limped down the stairs, he was already dressed in top hat and
formal clothes for his successor's swearing in. He carried an
umbrella that he planned to use as a cane if needed. Following
the ceremony and an informal luncheon in the rooms of the
Senate Committee on Naval Affairs, Cleveland and McKinley
returned to the White House and said good-bye. Cleveland left
by a side door. The day now belonged to McKinley alone. Cleveland was a private citizen once more.

In the meanwhile, the Clevelands had once again been house
hunting. Cleveland himself might have preferred to settle in
New York City again. But the growing family, he could see,
would flourish best in open spaces. Having visited Princeton,
New Jersey, he was enchanted by its beauty and quietude.
Shortly after the election, Cleveland had written to a professor
of classics, Andrew F. West (later to be dean of the graduate
school in fierce conflict with the Princeton president, Woodrow
Wilson), inquiring about the town and its virtues. Persuaded by
West of its outstanding merits, the Clevelands bought a large
colonial mansion that they named "Westland," in honor of the
friend who had brought them there.

In a short time Cleveland made himself a part of the Princeton
University community. Newspapers sometimes even called him
the Sage of Princeton. He managed remarkably to overcome his

sense of inferiority in the presence of scholars. Forgotten was the fact that he had refused honorary degrees from Harvard and Princeton in past years, and he now accepted one from Old Nassau in June 1897. Quickly becoming a fixture on the campus, he enjoyed his morning constitutional there. On afternoons when the weather was fair he would go for a ride with Frances in their carriage.

At commencements Cleveland had the privilege of marching in cap and gown at the head of the procession, alongside the president of Princeton, first Francis Patton, and, after 1902, Woodrow Wilson. Named a trustee of the university in 1903, he accepted his responsibility with his usual eagerness. He supported heartily the powers the trustees vested in Wilson to revamp the university. Inevitably, though, when the now-famous struggle developed between Dean West and President Wilson over the location of the new graduate school, Cleveland sided with his good friend. The bad blood that this created between Cleveland and Wilson, over what can only be called a minor academic issue, marred the relationship between the only two Democratic presidents elected between the outbreak of the Civil War and the onset of the Great Depression—and the only two such figures to live so close to each other on the grounds of a leading university.

When Cleveland left the presidency, he had a considerable nest egg—between $300,000 and $350,000. He could be called not rich, but well-to-do. This accumulation consisted of savings from his salary, earnings from his time as a lawyer, and the proceeds of the sale of Oak View. The money was securely invested for him by his old companion "Commodore" Benedict. Though not affluent, the Cleveland family was well provided for, and the ex-president had no financial need to seek employment. But he could not be idle. He soon was writing articles for a range of national magazines, including the *Atlantic,* the *Century,* and the *Ladies' Home Journal.* For his work he received substantial fees.

Like other former presidents, he wrote in the agreeable mood of reminiscence at the same time as he was unflinchingly defensive of the stands and decisions he had taken. In putting pen to paper, Cleveland may have had in mind Harrison's recent book, *This Country of Ours*, or even Buchanan's self-serving account of the secession crisis. The most famous of Cleveland's magazine pieces appeared in the *Saturday Evening Post* of May 7, 1904, its subject the Morgan gold deal, an event that had brought him much general opprobrium and continued to rankle in his heart. He summed up his presidential career in his book *Presidential Problems*, which was published the same year. It contains, along with this essay from the *Post*, his side of the Venezuela confrontation and the use of troops in the Pullman strike.

With his plentiful leisure time, he fished and hunted with friends, and at home he played billiards and cribbage. His intellectual horizon appeared to be no wider than it had ever been. The death of his firstborn, Ruth, was a devastating blow he never got over, although like other parents who have seen children die before themselves, he made a brave effort to overcome his grief when in the presence of Frances and the other children.

His correspondence from 1897 on shows his growing disappointment in McKinley's conduct of the presidency. Still a low-tariff man, he was appalled by the passage of the Dingley bill, which raised rates even higher. Then came the annexation of Hawaii in 1898, which he called "a perversion of our national mission."

The war against Spain was the coup de grâce. Athough he knew how much McKinley had tried to avoid it, he was anguished by the unfolding events. He wrote to Judson Harmon, who had been his last attorney general, that the death in battle and from disease of so many young men will make "thousands of American households dark" and lead to a "general and ominous inquiry as to the justification and necessity of this war."

When the Democrats renominated Bryan in 1900, Cleveland was at his crankiest and, as he told friends, in despair. He was apoplectic when he saw the gold Democrats willing to support Bryan because Bryan had declared imperialism to be the chief issue. Cleveland was still unforgiving of the silverites, and Bryan

was the chief among them. But if the party was no longer heed-
ing their former chief, as has happened often in American history,
he was none the less becoming the grand old man of American
politics. After McKinley's death by assassination—in Buffalo, of
all places, on September 14, 1901—Cleveland was the only living former president, Harrison having died the previous March.

In the dawn of the new century, Cleveland was already a
reminder of simpler days. He was no longer a partisan politician
but a beloved national treasure. He felt the change in public sentiment, and in 1904 he was pleased to stand with President
Theodore Roosevelt at the St. Louis Exposition to mark the centennial of the Louisiana Purchase. Still, he had been privately
critical of the administration's action in seizing Panama, seeing
it, as he had seen the annexation of Hawaii, as unworthy of
America's heritage.

Before the Democratic convention met in July and nominated
Alton B. Parker, chief justice of New York's highest court, some
newspapers were suggesting that the party draft Cleveland to run
for president once more. Of course, the flattering idea fell on deaf
ears, Cleveland's and those of most fellow Democrats. On election
night, the former president was dumbfounded by the overwhelm-
ing defeat that the uninspiring Parker suffered at the hands of
Roosevelt. Cleveland was not at home with the ebullient, swash-
buckling style of the Rough Rider, and he knew for sure that the
tone and tint of the nation he had once led were gone for good.

Cleveland's last public service was to involve himself in reorganizing the Equitable Life Assurance Society. Like other insurance companies, the Equitable had become the plaything of a
group of insiders who ran it for their benefit rather than for that
of the policyholders. In an effort to salvage the firm, Thomas
Fortune Ryan, who had become the majority stockholder, was
instrumental in persuading Cleveland to join the board of directors. Shortly, he was playing a major role in reshaping Equitable
and restoring the confidence of the insured. For his work, Cleveland was paid twelve thousand dollars—the only member of
the board to receive a fee. He was offered, and took a second

position for an additional twelve thousand dollars, the position as referee in disputes between insurance companies. He then accepted a post as head of the Association of Life Insurance Presidents at an annual salary of twenty-five thousand dollars. These connections were in keeping with his instinct to ally himself with conservative businessmen. Friends later suggested that, perhaps out of felt need for his youthful family, he had been lured by the emoluments. Alas, he seemed to have become a well-paid front man for the insurance industry. In fact, the sitting governor of New York, Charles Evans Hughes, played the decisive role in reorganizing the insurance industry, thereby earning him the reputation that would help make him the Republican nominee for president a few years later.

Cleveland's health had been declining for some years. He suffered from heart and kidney trouble that the doctors ascribed to his gastric difficulties and his recurrent bouts of gout. For some time he was sleeping with a stomach pump at hand. Still, he remained relatively active, speaking here and there, watching closely the doings of the White House, and attending to the responsibilities he had assumed. He had sold Gray Gables, out of fear that the Cape Cod Canal, shortly to be built, would destroy his bucolic vista. His friend John H. Finley, president of the College of the City of New York, introduced him to the still unspoiled mountain scenery of New Hampshire. The Clevelands fell in love with the region, and in 1906, acquired a house three miles from the village of Tamworth. They named it, appropriately, "Intermont." With their old-fashioned habits, they were unconcerned by being far from both a telegraph office or a railway line, or the fact that the nearest telephone was in the cottage of their property manager. They knew they would be dependent on horses for transportation.

Beginning in the fall of 1907, the ex-president grew more seriously ill, and in the following spring, he sensed he was a dying man. Sinking fast, he died on June 24 of a heart attack. His last words, it was reported, were: "I have tried so hard to do what is right." At his bedside stood his cherished Frank; his doctors, who had been hastily summoned, including his surgeon and friend Dr. James Bryant; and the ever-dependable William Sinclair, whom Mrs. Cleveland had sent for to help nurse her husband. The children were in Tamworth with Frances Cleveland's mother, Emma, now Mrs. Henry E. Perrine. The youngest, Francis Grover, five, and Richard, ten, remained there with her while the two eldest, Esther, fourteen, and Marion, twelve, hurried to Princeton to be with their mother.

The attendance at Cleveland's funeral was by invitation only. In addition to the immediate family, the select few included President Roosevelt, Chief Justice Fuller, and a number of favorite political associates. On June 26, following a simple service without ritual and marked only by the reading of passages from Scriptures, Cleveland was interred in the family plot in Princeton Cemetery alongside the grave of his daughter Ruth.

Epilogue

Cleveland lives in the national memory today almost exclusively as the president who had two nonconsecutive terms of office. He deserves a better fate, for he was once revered by millions of his contemporaries for genuine merits, especially integrity. They had seen virtue enough in him to accord him popular majorities in three presidential elections. He had the ill luck to be president in a time of rampant political corruption and of economic stringency for so many of his countrymen. The public understood that what the nation required, above all, was not brilliance but the cleansing honesty and straightforwardness that he provided. Though his was a gray personality, whose words were sometimes simple homilies more suited to the pulpit than the campaign trail, he exuded sincerity and decency. No one ever doubted what he meant or where he stood.

His career extended into the twentieth century, but his years in power were part of the horse-and-buggy era. He occupied a White House not yet fully lit by electricity, and he worked in a time when the president answered important mail himself and by hand. Many could see, though, that a different, more dynamic world was coming into being. For Americans it would be symbolized by a political style that placed the president at the center of a giant revolving stage, dominating it all like a top-hatted ringmaster. As a result, well before his life came to an end, Cleveland seemed an anachronism—very likely even to himself— but in his times the people idolized him for his principled fear- lessness in the role that the contingency of history gave him to play.

Milestones

March 18, 1837 Stephen Grover Cleveland born in Caldwell, N.J., to Richard Falley Cleveland and Ann Neal Cleveland.

1837 Princess Victoria crowned queen of England.

1844 The first telegraph line is completed—from Baltimore to Washington.

1846–48 The Mexican War results in the cession to the United States of California and the territory between Texas and California known as New Mexico.

1848 Revolutions convulse France, the Germanies, the Italies, and the Hapsburg Dominions.

1848 The discovery of gold in California sets off a gold rush.

1850 President Zachary Taylor dies in office. Millard Fillmore succeeds him and helps enact the Compromise of 1850.

1857 James Buchanan is inaugurated president and is fated to face the secession crisis.

1859 Charles Darwin publishes *The Origin of Species.*

1861 Lincoln is inaugurated president. The Civil War begins with the firing on Fort Sumter.

1863 Cleveland made assistant district attorney for Erie County, N.Y.

1863 The Battles of Vicksburg and Gettysburg take place.

1865   The Civil War ends. General Lee surrenders at Appomattox. Lincoln is assassinated.

November 1865   Cleveland is defeated in a run for district attorney.

1866   A telegraph cable is successfully laid across the Atlantic Ocean.

1868   Japan ends feudal government and restores the rule of the emperors.

1869   The first transcontinental railroad is completed with the joining of the Central Pacific and Union Pacific Railroads.

1870   The Franco-Prussian War results in France's defeat, the fall of Napoleon III, and the establishment of the Third French Republic.

The unification of Italy is completed and Rome becomes its capital with Victor Emmanuel II as king. The unification of Germany is completed and Wilhelm I is accepted as emperor.

The Vatican proclaims the dogma of papal infallibility.

1871   The Great Chicago Fire destroys the city.

1874   Queen Victoria is designated Empress of India.

1876   Alexander Graham Bell patents the telephone.

1876–77   President Rutherford B. Hayes is elected after a disputed canvass.

1879   Thomas A. Edison patents the incandescent electric lightbulb.

1881   President James A. Garfield is assassinated, and Chester A. Arthur becomes president.

Czar Alexander II is assassinated by terrorists.

November 1881   Cleveland is elected mayor of Buffalo.

November 1882   Cleveland is elected governor of New York.

1883–84   France completes its control over Indo-China.

July 8, 1884   Cleveland is nominated for president to run against the Republican James G. Blaine and is elected in November.

March 4, 1885   Cleveland's first term as president begins.

1885 Karl Benz in Germany produces the first automobile powered by an internal combustion engine.

June 2, 1886 Cleveland marries Frances Folsom at the White House.

1887 The United States acquires the right to establish a naval base at Pearl Harbor.

1888 Wilhelm II becomes emperor of Germany.

November 1888 Cleveland is defeated for reelection by Benjamin Harrison.

1889 Cleveland enters the private practice of law with the New York firm of Bangs, Stetson, Tracy and MacVeagh.

November 1892 Cleveland is reelected president, defeating Benjamin Harrison.

1894 The first public showing of a motion picture occurs—by the Lumière brothers in Paris.

The Dreyfus Affair erupts in France over a trumped-up charge of treason against a young captain.

1894–95 The Sino-Japanese War results in Japan's acquisition of Taiwan and other Chinese territories.

1895 Wilhelm C. Röntgen, in Germany, announces the discovery of X rays.

1896 The Democrats nominate William Jennings Bryan for president.

March 4, 1897 Cleveland's second term expires, and William McKinley becomes president.

1898 The United States annexes Hawaii.

The Spanish-American War ends with the United States acquiring colonial possessions: the Philippine Islands, Puerto Rico, and Guam.

1901 President McKinley is assassinated in Buffalo, and Theodore Roosevelt becomes president.

Queen Victoria dies and is succeeded by Edward VII, opening the Edwardian era.

Guglielmo Marconi sends the first wireless signals across the Atlantic.

1903 The Wright brothers successfully fly the first heavier-than-air aircraft.

1904–5 The Russo-Japanese War, with Japan victorious, discredits the czarist regime and generates public pressure for national reform.

1905 Albert Einstein propounds his theory of relativity.

1906 San Francisco is devastated by an earthquake.

June 24, 1908   Cleveland dies in Princeton, N.J.

Selected Bibliography

BY GROVER CLEVELAND

Presidential Problems (New York: The Century Company, 1904).
Fishing and Shooting Sketches (New York: Outing Publishing Company, 1906).
Good Citizenship (Philadelphia: Henry Altemus Company, 1908).

DOCUMENTS

Bergh, Albert Ellery, ed., *Grover Cleveland: Addresses, State Papers and Letters* (New York: The Sun Dial Classics Company, 1908).
Nevins, Allan, ed., *Letters of Grover Cleveland, 1850–1908* (New York: Houghton Mifflin Company, 1933).

BIOGRAPHICAL WORKS

Brodsky, Alyn, *Grover Cleveland: A Study in Character* (New York: St. Martin's Press, 2000).
Ford, Henry Jones, *The Cleveland Era: A Chronicle of the New Order in Politics* (New Haven: Yale University Press, 1919).
Gilder, Richard Watson, *Grover Cleveland: A Record of Friendship* (New York: The Century Company, 1910).

Hollingsworth, J. Rogers, *The Whirligig of Politics: The Democracy of Cleveland and Bryan* (Chicago: The University of Chicago Press, 1963).

Jeffers, H. Paul, *An Honest President: The Life and Presidencies of Grover Cleveland* (New York: William Morrow, 2000).

Lynch, Denis Tilden, *Grover Cleveland: A Man Four-Square* (New York: Horace Liveright, Inc., 1932).

McElroy Robert, *Grover Cleveland: The Man and the Statesman. An Authorized Biography*, 2 vols. (New York: Harper Brothers Publishers, 1923).

Merrill, Horace Samuel, *Bourbon Leader: Grover Cleveland and the Democratic Party* (Boston: Little, Brown & Co., 1957).

Nevins, Allan, *Grover Cleveland: A Study in Courage* (New York: Dodd, Mead & Co., 1944).

Summers, Mark Wahlgren, *Rum, Romanism, and Rebellion: The Making of a President, 1884* (Chapel Hill, N.C.: The University of North Carolina Press, 2000).

Tugwell, Rexford Guy, *Grover Cleveland* (New York: The Macmillan Co., 1968).

Welch, Richard E., Jr., *The Presidencies of Grover Cleveland* (Lawrence, Kan.: University Press of Kansas, 1988).

CAMPAIGN BIOGRAPHIES (IN CHRONOLOGICAL ORDER)

Triplett, Frank, *The Authorized Pictorial Lives of Stephen Grover Cleveland and Thomas Andrew Hendricks* (Cincinnati: Cincinnati Publishing Company, 1884).

Welch, Deshler, *Stephen Grover Cleveland: A Sketch of His Life* (New York: J. W. Lovell Co., 1884).

Goodrich, Frederick K., *The Life and Public Services of Grover Cleveland* (Portland, Maine: H. Hallett and Co., 1884).

Hensel, W. U., *Life and Public Services of Grover Cleveland and Allen G. Thurman* (Philadelphia: Hubbard Brothers, Publishers, 1888).

Shepp, James W., *Life of Grover Cleveland . . . and Adlai E. Stevenson* (Philadelphia: Political Publishing Co., 1892).

Index

ABOUT THE AUTHOR

———

Henry F. Graff is a professor emeritus of history at Columbia University, where he taught his pioneering seminar on the presidency. The author of *The Tuesday Cabinet* and the standard reference work *The Presidents*, among other books, he is a frequent commentator on radio and television. He and his wife live in Scarsdale, New York.